When Music

DIV|DES
THE CHURCH

James Michael Riccitelli

Published by

H&E Berk
Blissfield, Michigan

James M. Riccitelli
The Berean Fellowship
4212 Onondaga
Toledo, Ohio 43611
419-537-0661 or 419-729-0733
Fax 419-729-9939

ISBN 0-9658900-0-7

Cover Design by Kenda M. Riccitelli

Published by

H&E Berk

208 South Lane Street
Blissfield, Michigan 49228

CONTENTS

Acknowledgements

This book grew out of my heart's desire to see unity prevail both within and among churches that confess Jesus Christ as Lord and Savior. In 1967, I began sensing the possibility of a crisis over church music that might divide churches as theology had done in the past. To this end I took the unusual step—I was over 40—of enrolling at the University of Toledo (Ohio) for a bachelor's degree and subsequently for a master's degree (both in Sociology) on condition that I would be allowed to write a thesis on the social setting of rock and roll. It seemed to me that understanding the counter-culture and its new musical style was imperative.

A number of professors were very helpful in guiding me through the research and writing of the thesis. These included Dr. L. Noel Moyer, Dr. Ruth Searles and Dr. Sidney Kaplan—all of the Department of Sociology, Anthropology and Social Work—and Dr. Arthur Winsor of the Department of Music. Other professors at the University and instructors at local high schools opened their classrooms for the collecting of data.

As the bibliography will show, I am deeply indebted to many others who have touched on the subject one way or another. Some of my basic ideas and hypotheses took shape before I was exposed to Dr. Francis Schaeffer, whose marvelous works helped affirm the direction I was taking.

I must thank the leaders of my local church where I have served as pastor for over two decades; they have been gracious in allowing me a forum to discuss many of these ideas as well as time to coax these ideas into written form.

I am grateful to those who have looked over the manuscript of this book and offered ideas and comments. Especially am I thankful for the encouragement of Dr. Robert Webber of Wheaton College, Wheaton, Illinois, and for my friend and colleague, Dr. Harold Berk, who permitted me opportunities to teach at William Tyndale College in Farmington Hills, Michigan, while he was Academic Dean, and who now serves as my publisher. His help has been invaluable.

The biggest bouquet must go to my wife, Ruth, who has made my working conditions as pleasant as possible. She has endured my stubbornness in keeping at this project for so many years as I attempted to make sense of the mountain of research I had collected—all the while pastoring a growing church. Her unselfish pouring out of herself and support of my ministry and work are indescribable gifts of love.

To the glory of God
and
to Ruth,
my Proverbs Thirty-one wife,
my co-laborer in ministry,
and my friend,
I dedicate this book
with love

Preface

Americans love music as radio, television programming and the extraordinary sales of audio cassettes and CDs across the land attest. We're not alone in love of music. Music is found in every culture.

The book of Psalms reveals the Israelites were a musical people, too. King David created choirs and a temple orchestra. Certain families were chosen to lead music and teach it to succeeding generations. The psalms exhorted the Jews to "Sing to the Lord *a new song.*"

Music has always been a part of the church and its worship. Evangelicals love music and it is difficult to imagine a church service without it! However, there is evidence that music is dividing today's evangelical churches. Why should this be? Division in the past resulted from differences of opinion over theology. Today, churches are breaking up over differences in musical styles. A particular musical style at the center of much of the controversy found in evangelical churches today is 'rock and roll' or more simply, rock. Can the church put its stamp of approval on this style?

The present crisis can be traced back to the counter-culture with its germination in the 1950's and its adoption of rock. Many proponents in today's evangelical church endorse rock groups and rock concerts billed as *Christian.* Its introduction in evangelical churches often results in polarization and division, principally between younger folk and the senior generation. Some churches offer two Sunday morning services, one billed as 'contemporary' if they use rock or rock-like music and the other as 'traditional' if they do not.

How can we avoid church division over musical styles and worship programming? We must look at the rock musical style as carefully and as dispassionately as possible. Rock is complex. To understand it requires considerable analysis and reflection.

Rock *is* music, music is an art form, and art forms and styles have a close connection with a people's culture. Music is a "universal language" only in the most general sense; that musical styles are generally not transcultural is a proposition critical to this study— *music reflects or mirrors culture as well as reinforces it.* A study of

7

the musical style of a culture will tell us something about that culture's ideas and world view.

It may surprise us to learn that the counter-culture actually proposed some positive values and corrective measures. When they were rejected, the counter-culture prophesied doom. To make its point, the counter-culture resorted to extreme methods and as a result, positive values offered by the counter-culture were subordinated to negative ones.

The real surprise comes when we find that our own culture has been adopting the counter-culture's positive values wholesale and with a vengeance, but with no more balance than existed in the society before the movement began.

A culture needs balance in positive, *paired values*—a concept explored in this study. If there is appreciation for balance, musical styles will reflect that balance. If there isn't, musical styles will not only reflect imbalanced *extreme values*, but will also *reinforce* them!

Framing this central core of study about the counter-culture with its rock musical style reflecting its world view, is first, a brief survey of music in the Bible and church history with special emphasis on change and its effect on the church, and lastly, practical guidelines based on conclusions drawn from the study.

Whether we are pragmatically or aesthetically oriented, the result of this plan of study will allow us to discern if rock musical style is useful in worship and evangelistic services, and if so, to what degree. It will also allow for conclusions based on reason rather than just personal feelings. Above all, there will result a more peaceful spirit within a local church trying to handle change.

Since music incites powerful emotions, the reader is urged to work through the material from the beginning and resist turning directly to the suggested guidelines. The result will be a more sympathetic appreciation for the complexity of the subject while discovering important clues for developing consensus and practical guidelines. An in-depth analysis of the counter-culture will also allow for a better understanding of the mind of 'boomers' and 'busters' and thus make evangelism and edification more effective.

James M. Riccitelli
Toledo, Ohio

What's Going On Here?

The old order changeth, yielding place to new.
The Passing of Arthur *(1869), Alfred Lord Tennyson*

I had to stand for forty minutes during a song service," said a surprised older gentleman after attending a worship service at a church he had not visited before. He added with indignation, "And some of those choruses were sung repeatedly!" His legs, his heart, and his mind all disapproved. He, a churchgoer for many decades, had been distracted in worship by such changes and downright disturbed in his spirit!

Wasn't he right and they wrong? Or was it the other way around? Having lived a few decades myself, his remark caused me to remember a typical evangelical church practice which he forgot. And what was that? He forgot about the 'invitation hymn' sung at the close of an evangelistic service when a congregation stood fifteen or more minutes while the invitation was given to sinners to come forward. Repetition? The stanzas of the same hymn were sung over and over.

Several years ago, I attended a ministerium meeting at a church location that I had not before visited. The exterior of the modest building was traditional in architecture. After stepping into the sanctuary and looking around, I couldn't help but inquire, "Where's the pulpit?" The pastor replied with a smile, "Oh, we put that out in the shed; we don't need it because we all sit in a circle." I wasn't sure whether I should have said, "Amen!" to that or offered to pray for the younger pastor!

It doesn't take much observation these days to conclude that there are radical changes taking place in contemporary church architecture, furnishings, worship style and especially music. If pulpits are not removed, we may find a clear Lucite one. In some sanctuaries one may be hard put to find a piano, organ, or a hymnal; they have all been stored. We also find praise choruses in place of hymns, 'worship leaders' instead of 'songleaders,' words projected on screens freeing hands to be raised during the long song service (now labeled 'worship'), and handclapping.

Historically, church splits resulted from doctrinal differences. Today church splits occur because of differences over worship style—and especially over the musical style used in worship.

A thoughtful Christian might ask, "Has an important part of worship been rediscovered?" Another might ask, "Has something alien to worship been introduced?" The introduction of change slowly is always advisable, but the conclusion as to what is legitimate change for evangelical congregations requires diligent study and heart sensitivity.

Call for the 'New'

The church that would escape change had better relocate on the moon. Change is knocking insistently on the door. Nor will it go away with inattentiveness. If leaders are turning a deaf ear to such changes, many congregants are not.

Some Christians have strong ties to the traditional because there is a sense of security promoted by changelessness. Scriptures urges us to *remember*. Long-time church members may view change as blasphemy. Others find excitement in trying something new, urged on by a growing suspicion the 'old' is actually worn out.

The concept of 'new' is biblical as well. God commands believers in not a few places to "sing a *new* song" (Psalms 33:3, 40:3, 96:1, 98:1, 101:1, 144:9; Isaiah 42:10). In the book of Revelation, St. John said believers will sing a new song before the throne of God.

What is the *new song* Christians are to sing? The Psalmist tells us that it is "a hymn of praise" (40:3), a "shout of joy" (98:4,6), a song of His "love and justice" (101:1), a song of "victory" (144:9-10), and a means whereby His praise is conveyed "in the assembly of the saints." Since the Lord's mercies are "new every morning" (Lamentations 3:22-23), there is no end to the praise God's people may offer Him in speech and in song. Every Christian believer should have a new song to sing about the Lord's mercies at the close of every day!

There is no argument about the exhortation; the question is rather *how* shall we praise the Lord in song?

Reynolds and Price tell us, "Christian song is never static, never quite the same from one generation to another."[1]

Today the call is to sing more about God in Scriptural terms, and the renewed emphasis on the biblical psaltery (the book of Psalms) is commendable if not a bit out of balance (e.g., where are the new songs about the person and work of Jesus Christ, and especially about His resurrection?). And the call by many younger folks is to bring the rock musical style into church services.

Is the hymnal not enough? Charles H. Kraft, professor of anthropology and intercultural communication at Fuller Theological Seminary addressed that question in a short article published by *Christianity Today* in the late 1980's. The article was titled, "The Hymnal Is Not Enough." He wrote:

> While I have always enjoyed singing in the church, it wasn't until I freed myself from exclusive use of the hymnal that I experienced what praise and worship can be. And it is the new music, sung with eyes closed for 10, 15, or 20 minutes at a time, that makes the experience possible. These short, repetitious songs help me focus on God; I don't even need to look at the music.[2]

This writer tells us that singing helps him "focus on God" and these "short, repetitious songs" enhance worship. He implies that the hymnal was tried and found wanting. True, hymns are not "short and repetitious" because they were intended to be a source of teaching doctrine. Are we to accede to his argument that these short, repetitious songs of praise are better because they help us focus on God whereas hymns do not? Are we to accept his contention that unless one is freed from exclusive use of the hymnal, one cannot focus on God?

Many agree with Kraft's view while others vigorously reject it believing that compromise, heresy, and even blasphemy are appropriate counter-charges.

The hymn focuses the mind on God, while the new worship or praise choruses sung repetitively focus one's feelings on God. Is one better than the other? Is either one better without the other? Is this change for the better, for the worse, or merely change for change's sake because we are just plain tired of the old? One line in an early *Madrigal* by an anonymous fifteenth century composer says, "All things change except the love of change."³

Help, Lord! Where do we go from here?

Shaking up the Comfortable

Why does change come with labor pains? To appreciate the difficulty of change, we do well to remember that tradition is not just a logical set of ideas. Tradition is drenched in emotion.

An older gentleman was invited to a joint service in another church facility of the same denomination. He soon found there was no altar rail in the beautiful new multi-million dollar facility. When the reality sank in, he began to shake his head in disbelief saying, "Where's the altar rail? I was saved at an altar rail forty years ago!" He was very uncomfortable!

Church v. Secular Music

In the late 1960's I attended a National Religious Broadcasters' regional conference in Chicago. Two musicians who were often featured on Moody Bible Institute's radio station, WMBI, and at the Moody Church in Chicago, hosted one of the sessions and introduced the conference to what they believed was the trend in Christian musical styles. They played two hymns for the conference and one was the gospel song, "Higher Ground."⁴ The style, however, was that of the big band sound of the 1940's.

One of the delegates whom I judged to be in his late thirties or early forties stood up and voiced his disapproval with a tone that was unmistakably that of one offended: "I *danced* to that sound before I became a Christian!" He believed there was a line between secular and Christian music, and these selections were over the line. To him, it was unacceptable on the grounds of association. The two men leading the seminar, Bill Pearce and Larry Mayfield, were prophets, for, right or wrong, that sound is now common fare over Christian radio stations.

Traditionally, it was assumed there was a difference between church and secular music. This trend challenged that assumption. But it also raised serious questions. With these trends, I thought, "Tomorrow, would we be hearing 'Christian hard rock' and

'Christian heavy metal?'" My thoughts were certainly on target! I wondered, "Are there no boundaries or limits?" Perhaps music is music. . . is music. . . is music. . . Is musical style nothing more than personal preference?

If we have a category known as 'church music' will there be a sameness to all the tunes? "Will it be a style that lacks creativity?" as a friend once asked. My response was that there is no one more creative than God, and if His children are composing *godly* church music it ought to be characterized by all kinds of variety!

Posture in Worship

Many years ago, a woman said, "Pastor, I am having difficulty with your services." The problem sounded serious. "What disturbs me," she explained, "is the hymn-singing." I listened intently as she continued, "I am used to *standing* every time the congregation sings a hymn, and you don't have the people stand." She had not come from a charismatic congregation where standing and singing often go together, but from a more formal, liturgical church where worshipers always stood to sing hymns from the hymnal in the Sunday morning worship hour. With her, it became habit somehow tied in with spirituality. Is there a spiritual posture?

The evangelical pastor of another mainline denominational church invited me to be a guest speaker for a Lenten service. Midway through the service, ushers distributed a sheet of 'praise choruses' to the congregation. At the appropriate moment in the service the 'worship leader' directed the congregation to sing through the choruses without further announcement. "Of course," the leader emphasized, "*we will have to stand to sing.*" I took from his tone of voice that it would have been unacceptable worship to have remained seated.

One charismatic church leader told of the time he had opportunity to visit Africa and be part of a service where there was a great crowd of people. He says they stood for close to two hours and sang a single, simple song with two lines to the lyrics. The words went something like this:

> *Have you followed Jesus?*
> *I did.*

He concluded, "When they finished singing, there were no unbelievers left in the crowd." Whether he meant everyone got converted or unbelievers gave up in puzzlement and went home is not certain.

Handclapping

In the mid-nineteen seventies, a young married man delighted me by asking if he could share something with me from the Scriptures. It gladdens a pastor's heart to know members of his congregation are studying the Word on their own. He was about to suggest some change, and I had no problem with that. He shared Psalm 47:1, "O clap your hands, all ye people; shout unto God with the voice of triumph."

Then he gave me cause for concern by adding, "When we worship, we must clap our hands." He added to my consternation, "This is a command according to this psalm." I was a bit taken back. *"Must?"* My mind raced to the "Old Hundredth" tune that we commonly use for the Doxology and to "Holy, Holy, Holy" and other similar hymns. How would clapping make those hymns more worshipful? How would a congregation even clap to such hymns?

I am not opposed to handclapping. For a dozen years, my wife and I lived in Burkina Faso (formerly Upper Volta), West Africa, as missionaries. We were encouraged to introduce hand-clapping to African Christians as an accompaniment for singing by The Christian and Missionary Alliance Area Secretary for Africa, Rev. George Constance, who himself had served previously as a missionary to South America. He visited a local church service with us on the field and discovered the Bwa (formerly Red Bobo) church did not use any instruments, nor did they clap to accompany their singing.

The first generation of Christians did not feel they could associate with the native musical instruments (principally drums and an xylophone-like instrument called the balaphone) because of their close association with fetish worship and obscenity. Hand-clapping turned out to be a great asset in singing while trying to deal with the problem caused by the loss of instrumental accompaniment. The Bwa loved handclapping while singing, and the change proved to be a blessing to the church.

Later, we introduced percussion-type instruments imported from England, including cymbals, musical sleigh bells, a triangle and a tambourine. The tambourine was an instant success and in time, home-made tambourine-like instruments began to appear. The next generation of Christians developed a new style of drum.

Returning to my friend and his view of Psalm 47:1, I must report his comments puzzled me. I was not sure why he was troubled since, in the very church he attended, the congregants often clapped their hands while singing. Now he seemed to be saying that he had found a scriptural basis for the notion of *must:* "When we sing, we *must* clap our hands!"

Clap for *all* songs? As I mulled over his exhortation, my first need was to understand what Psalm 47 was saying. I began thinking out loud as I answered my friend. "Psalms are poetry," I said. "Is hand-clapping here just a figure of speech?" He replied instantly but not unkindly, "I knew you were going to suggest that."

I tried another line of thought. "If we must clap, then to be consistent with this verse, we must also shout, for the verse says, "Clap your hands, all ye people; *shout* unto God with the voice of triumph." He thought that was probably true, but he was not ready to insist on shouting.

I researched the question in Scripture and found handclapping and shouting in the Hebrew culture originally had to do with the coronation of a king. The first instance is found in Second Kings where we read:

> Jehoiada brought out the king's son and put the crown on him; he presented him with a copy of the covenant and proclaimed him king. They anointed him, and the people clapped their hands and shouted, "Long live the king!"[5]

Psalm 98:8 contains the phrase, "Let the rivers clap their hands. . ." which is obviously poetic, but the theme of the group of Psalms from 93 to 99 has to do with the King and His kingdom: "The Lord reigns!" The theme of Psalm 47 is the coronation of Messiah as King, so hand-clapping is consistent with this occurrence.

Clapping had other social functions among the Jews, one of which, when connected with hissing (Job 27:23), implies rejection of an authority figure or unseating a leader (we would call it impeachment). After this explanation, my friend and his family left the church to join one he felt was more consistent with his preference. Happily, we continued to regard one another warmly as brothers in the Lord.

Are certain physical movements or gestures a must for proper worship or are they a matter of personal preference?

Attendance Rationale

One approach for promoting contemporary music is the attendance argument since this up-beat, happy and more informal worship style attracts people, especially younger people. "If it attracts young people, isn't that sufficient justification for using the new worship style?" goes one argument. Americans cherish 'what works' and success is generally viewed as having something to do with increasing numbers. And if it attracts young people who are "the future church," is that not sufficient justification?

This can be countered with another argument. "If it offends and repels older people, isn't that sufficient justification for *not* using it?" The exodus of younger people from traditional churches was—and should be—of great concern to the church. Today, there is an exodus of older people from traditional-turned-contemporary-churches. That should be of equal concern to the church.

The attendance argument has not been lost on pastors of traditional evangelical churches who see this new 'worship style' as a God-sent answer to declining attendance. But there is no benefit in solving one distressing problem by replacing it with another equally distressing problem!

Worship: Why? and How?

Why we worship is a question addressed in Scriptures. *How* we worship is addressed only indirectly since the 'how' has something to do with culture and symbols. We know we are to pray, and we are told why in the Word. One cannot make a case, however, for an exclusive gesture or posture for prayer. In the Bible, God's people stood, knelt, lifted their arms to heaven, and fell on their faces in prayer. The basic New Testament exhortation is, "Pray continually"[6] and the body posture is left to the individual.

Rabbis instruct Jewish men to wear a prayer shawl, a small head-covering, and to bob the head up and down in visible assent. The 'how' of prayer for Muslims is to bow with their forehand touching the ground while facing towards Mecca, and that only after a ritual bathing. The Bwa of Burkina Faso coined a word to describe Muslim praying by making the noun 'forehead' into a verb, 'to forehead,' indicating the Muslim posture in prayer.

A fundamental requirement is for a church to review its practices and in painful honesty separate doctrine from methods. It will hurt. It is well to remember, however, that it is not wrong to do things because it has been the custom to do those things for many decades even when there is no other justification than, "This is our custom." It is also very right to re-examine those practices to make sure they have not become self-serving or tests of spirituality.

While a missionary in Africa, I devoted some of my time to the formation of the native hymnody and suggested on one occasion to my older missionary colleagues that since many of the tribes in French West Africa (the area I was familiar with) were pentatonic in musical scale—a five-tone scale similar to the five black notes on the piano—and the music in our American hymnals is written using seven tones, our Western hymn tunes ought to be rearranged to accommodate this cultural factor. This is not as novel a thought as it seems. A quick check in my French language hymnal showed American gospel songs were put into the French hymns with some musical rearrangement.

The explosion probably was not heard in the next county, but there was a negative reaction to altering any hymn tune which, to some, ranked in inspiration right next to the Bible.

After I published an article on the subject for a Christian anthropology journal, a missionary working in Burma wrote to the editor criticizing me for suggesting that the hymns written by Adoniram Judson were no good! I did no such thing, but it appears I somehow cast reflection on this great missionary pioneer's work by suggesting hymn-tune adaptation.

One Christian musicologist left the distinct impression during a public lecture which I attended that raising hands and falling down were part of biblical worship. He implied clearly that it was therefore mandatory if believers were to worship God truly. To some, this is methodology; to him, it was theology.

Is worship somehow better without instruments which have been associated with jazz or rock, such as saxophones, guitars and drums? Or, is a service more worshipful because they are used? The younger folk in some churches demand the use of guitars, drums and keyboards and disparage what older folks cherish—organs and pianos.

In some evangelical churches it is 'theologically incorrect' to play secular classical music; even Bach who wrote music for the church would receive a very cool reception. In the late 1940's, a teenager shared with me that the leadership of his small evangelical church asked him to play his violin for a service, but when they found out he had selected "Minuet in G," they refused to let him play.

In other churches, classical music is welcomed while gospel songs of the "Power in the Blood" variety are not. Who is right? Who is wrong? Why has this come to either/or?

New methods in worship include the addition of wonderfully sophisticated and powerful sound systems. Unfortunately, they are often manned by audio technicians who crank the sound up and give the impression (intentionally or not) that the louder we bang on our drums, strike our cymbals, or bellow out our songs, the greater the praise. It brings to mind the sarcasm of Elijah to the prophets of Baal:

> At noon Elijah began to taunt them, "Shout louder!" he said, "Surely he is a god! Perhaps he is deep in thought, or busy, or traveling. Maybe he is sleeping and must be awakened." So they shouted louder. . .[7]

Electronics can enhance musical sound powerfully, but technicians can make the music appeal more to the emotions than the mind or will by cranking up the accompaniment and obscuring lyrics. These days, who has not been exposed to music where the soloist's message was drowned out by the accompaniment? Sound that bathes and overwhelms hardly qualifies as a guarantee for better worship.

When that musical style is brought into the church as a means to worship, is the euphoria or ecstasy produced by it 'of the Spirit'? Or, has the 'how' obscured the 'what' and the 'why' by indulging in emotional excess? These are questions we shall address in later chapters.

Is It Edification?

The primary test of appropriateness for any change in the church is not whether one leaves worship feeling good, but rather, does it edify (build up)? This is the one thing St. Paul sets forth as a requirement when the church meets together.[8] Edification suggests a rational component.

Does that mean all emotions are to be left outside the church door before entering? Of course not. St. Peter's sermon on the day of Pentecost stirred up emotions; his listeners were "cut to the heart" and in great distress.[9] There is no biblical justification in denying public expression of feelings in worship.

A number of years ago, an underground Seattle newspaper, *Helix*, printed a rave review of an acid rock group called The Doors.[10] In his work, *The Making of the Counter-Culture,* Theodore Roszak quotes this graphic review and suggests it should not come as a surprise that after such events "a fretful call for *rationality* should be raised:"

> The Doors. Their style has overtones of the Massacre of the Innocents. An electrified sex slaughter. A music bloodbath. . . The Doors are carnivores in a land of musical vegetarians. . . Their talons, fangs, and fold wings are seldom out of view, but if they leave us crotch-raw and exhausted, at least they leave us aware of our aliveness. And of our destiny. The Doors scream into the darkened auditorium what all of us in the underground are whispering more softly in our hearts: We want the world and we want it. . . NOW![11]

The line between frenzy and true religious ecstasy is easily blurred, and with examples like this account of the Doors, the senior generation can hardly be blamed for being apprehensive about cranking up the emotions in worship services.

In the early nineteenth century, spirituality was measured in some churches by the 'holy laugh.' The practice blurred the true meaning of spirituality and happily soon passed.[12] This practice has been revived in the 1990s, but should come as no surprise given our renewed emphasis on and acceptance of the public display of emotions.

The test of whether a gift is truly from the Holy Spirit or a counterfeit gift from the adversary centers around this issue: does its practice edify?

Safeguards

One church leader, not skilled in music, asked, "What are the safeguards to keep us from being led in the wrong direction?" When should we shift into high gear? When should we put on the brakes?

Unfortunately when it comes to music, we have little to fall back on other than personal preference expressed in the words "I know what I like!" This implies that what I like is right and good but for no reason other than, "I like it!" The reasoning (if that's the proper word, and I doubt that it is) goes like this: "Since I like it and I am a sincere Christian, it follows that it must be good, right and therefore spiritual." It does not.

What is 'must'? What is compromise? What is optional? We must examine these issues and find appropriate boundaries if we are to develop safeguards. Can there be boundaries in the arts? Surely, say some, the arts must be allowed to be totally free—absolutely spontaneous, reasoning that whatever is art must be good simply because it is art. Spontaneous creativity with no boundaries whatsoever? That actually is a definition of cancer.

When all is said and done, believers need to know what is 'must' (this is foundational for spirituality), what is compromise (this is antithetical to spirituality), and what is personal preference (optional but still subject to the law of love[13]).

More Questions

Admittedly, what constitutes the 'right' music for worship is complex. Personal and cultural preferences make it confusing. There are many more questions Christians should ask before drawing conclusions. The danger is that proponents of contemporary music (rock and rock-like) tend to close their minds and say, "I like the music, kids get saved in rock concerts, so what is there to discuss?" Equally a danger is the perspective of those who have already rejected the musical style, saying "I can't identify with the music, I don't like it, so what is there to discuss?" I plead for an open mind and a humbleness of spirit that is willing to put aside personal feelings until all the data is reviewed.

Here is a list of more fundamental questions leadership should be asking and we shall address these in subsequent chapters:

> *What major musical changes have occurred in church history?*
>
> *How has the church handled change over the centuries?*
>
> *Does a more formal worship hinder the Spirit's wooing?*
>
> *Does the more informal worship violate the Lord's command to do everything 'decently and in order'?*
>
> *How do we find balance in church music? Is an eclectic worship style impossible?*
>
> *Is there such a thing as 'Christian music' and, if so, what is it?*
>
> *How has the counter-culture and rock music impacted the church?*
>
> *Are there Christian principles to guide us?*

Questions, questions, and more questions! Are there any truly Christian answers? I believe so, but the quest for answers requires diligent pursuit. There is no short-cut if one wishes a truly biblical solution.

2

Silver Trumpets, Rams' Horns and Tambourines

The trumpeters and singers joined in unison as with one voice, to give praise and thanks to the Lord. Accompanied by trumpets, cymbals and other instruments, they raised their voices in praise to the Lord and sang: "He is God; his love endures forever." Then the temple of the Lord was filled with a cloud, and the priests could not perform their service because of the cloud, for the cloud of the Lord filled the temple of God.

At the dedication of the first temple, Jerusalem, c. 1004 B.C.[1]

In one church where the musicians were experimenting with a tambourine, the word was quietly whispered about, "Hide that thing when the musicians aren't looking!" In another church, the musicians wouldn't begin until the tambourine was found. Whether we are used to the tambourine sound along with our worship or not, the instrument had Moses' blessing.

On the other hand, it may come as a shock to those who pride themselves in worshiping God in a fashion they view as literally paralleling Scripture when they learn there is no mention of drums in the Bible. Does this make the usage of drums in worship wrong? I doubt that. There is no mention of the organ (as we know it) nor of the piano in the Bible either. Nor of the double bass, nor of the oboe.

The Bible doesn't deal directly with many of the questions raised today about music in worship, but it doesn't deal directly with many social issues either. However, there are answers—*there must be answers*—if the Bible is to function truly as our guide for faith and living. First, we will make a search of the Old Testament to learn what we can about music used in worship. Here are some questions to guide us along in our search:

What does the Old Testament tell us about singers and instru-
   mentalists?
What did King David have to say about this?
What was the Temple orchestra like?
What was the significance to clapping and shouting in the Old
   Testament?
What about using tambourines and drums?
Is greater volume greater worship?

Early Use

Music is as ancient as the book of Genesis in which we read,
"Jubal was the father of all who play the harp and flute" (4:21 NIV).
The book of Exodus mentions a praise-gathering where Israelites
came together to celebrate the overthrow of Pharaoh's army. That
account reveals that tambourines were in use at the time: "Then
Miriam the prophetess, Aaron's sister, took a tambourine in her
hand, and all the women followed her, with tambourines and dancing" (15:20 NIV).

Jubal and Miriam were among the first recorded instrumental-
ists. Women, it should be noted, played tambourines (or 'timbrels'
as some translations have it), as the stories of Miriam and Jephthah's
daughter make clear.[2]

The use of music to calm the spirit is noted in the book of First
Samuel. The record tells us an evil spirit was permitted by the Lord
to afflict King Saul. A person capable of playing the harp was sought
to play for King Saul when he was so afflicted. They found David,
an accomplished musician, who later became king in Saul's place.
The account concludes, "Whenever the spirit from God came upon
Saul, David would take his harp and play. Then relief would come
to Saul; he would feel better, and the evil spirit would leave him."[3]
In this century, science 'discovered' that musical therapy has positive effects on the mind. The Bible said it first!

Elsewhere in the Old Testament, we find additional "songs"
such as the Song of Moses (Exodus 15, Deuteronomy 31:30f), the
Song of Deborah (Judges 5), and the Song of Solomon (an entire
book of eight chapters). The text of these songs are generally in
poetry form.

In the Old Testament, singing is mentioned as early as Moses' day and as late as Nehemiah's time when the returned exiles celebrated the rebuilding of the wall in Jerusalem (c. 430 B.C.). Worshipers coming to Jerusalem for the holy festivals chanted the *Hallel,* meaning 'Praise' (Psalms 113-118), a tradition that continued till Jesus' day. There were temple choirs who sang in unison, antiphonally, and perhaps in parts.

The longest book in the Bible, The Psalms, is in reality a songbook filled with hymns that touch on every emotion of human experience while directing the spirit toward praise and worship of a sovereign Lord. The songs in this hymnal, written by a number of writers, exhort worshipers to praise and glorify God with singing.[4] It was the hymnal of the second temple.[5] Unfortunately, none of the musical accompaniments has been preserved, although Hebrew words are found in a few of the Psalms which may indicate either a tune or a musical notation, such as, *gittith, mahalath leannoath, maskil, selah,*[6] etc. The actual meaning of these words is unclear.

David's Contribution

David, the songwriter-king, encouraged the formation of both choirs and orchestras. Davis says of David,

> [He] was assisted in his work by Asaph, Heman, and Ethan or Jeduthun, three masters of music. A choir of singers and musicians with Asaph at its head, was formed of Levites, and stationed before the ark at the tabernacle on Zion, while Heman and Jeduthun, with their choirs were assigned to the old tabernacle at Gibeon (I Chron. 16:4-6, 39-42). These three choirs were afterwards united in the temple. In David's reign they numbered 4,000 members (I Chron. 23:5), of whom 288 were trained musicians, who were depended upon to lead the less skilled body of assistants (I Chron. 25:7,8). They were divided into twenty-four courses, containing twelve trained musicians each. . . [In Herod's] temple a choir of boys, standing at the foot of the stairs [which led from the court of Israel to the court of the priests], lent their higher voices to the song of the Levites.[7]

When King David decided to bring the ark up from the house of Obed-Edom to Jerusalem, we are told in I Chronicles 15 he appointed a choir to accompany the procession: "David told the leaders of the Levites to appoint their brothers as singers to sing joyful songs, accompanied by musical instruments: lyres, harps and cymbals."[8] The text continues with the details:

> The musicians Heman, Asaph and Ethan were to sound the bronze cymbals; Zechariah, Aziel, Shemiramoth, Jehiel, Unni, Eliab, Maaeseiah and Benaiah were to play the lyres according to *alamoth,* and Mattithiah, Eliphelehu, Mikneiah, Obed-Edom, Jeiel and Azaziah were to play the harps according to *sheminith.* Kenaniah the head Levite was in charge of the singing; that was his responsibility because he was skilled at it.[9]

In the next chapter, after the ark of God was brought safely and joyously to Jerusalem, David appointed what appears to be a more permanent orchestra "to minister before the ark of the Lord, to make petition, to give thanks, and to praise the Lord, the God of Israel." This list differs slightly from the above orchestra and choir:

> Asaph was the chief, Zechariah second, then Jeiel, Shemiramoth, Jehiel, Mattithiah, Eliab, Benaiah, Obed-Edom and Jeiel. They were to play the lyres and harps, Asaph was to sound the cymbals, and Benaiah and Jahaziel the priests were to blow the trumpets regularly before the ark of the covenant of God.[10]

David requested Asaph and his associates to minister before the ark of the covenant of the LORD regularly, according to each day's requirements. He also commanded Obed-Edom and his sixty-eight associates to minister with them.[11]

Lyrics were clearly heard above David's temple orchestra[12] given what we are told about the composition of that musical group. In Herod's temple, there were ordinarily two psalteries [lyres], nine harps, and one cymbal, and on certain days pipes [flutes[13]] were added. What about the cymbals and trumpets? The use of the cymbals is curious, but since it is a percussion instrument, it may have been struck by the chief musician to beat time. The participation of priests with trumpets along with the orchestra of stringed instruments occurred, but seemed to be exceptional (2 Chronicles 5:12,13; 7:6). In the second temple, the musicians stood on the east of the great altar (2 Chronicles 5:12)[14]; silver trumpets and the less melodic shofar trumpets, when blown in connection with the regular orchestra, were heard in the pauses or as responsive music (Ezra 3:10,11). There was no ambiguity in the message of praise; there was order—not confusion.

Additional details concerning the singers in the temple as commanded by King David are recorded in 1 Chronicles 25:1ff (NIV):

> David, together with the commanders of the army, set apart some of the sons of Asaph, Heman and Jeduthun for the ministry of prophesying, accompanied by harps, lyres and cymbals. Here is the list of the men who performed this service. . .

The list that follows in the text includes four of Asaph's sons "who prophesied under the king's supervision," six of Jeduthun's sons "who prophesied, using the harp in thanking and praising the Lord," and fourteen of Heman's sons who "were given him through the promises of God to exalt him." The account continues:

> All these men were under the supervision of their fathers for the music of the temple of the Lord, with cymbals, lyres and harps, for the ministry at the house of God. Asaph, Jeduthun and Heman were under the supervision of the king. Along with their relatives—all of them trained and skilled in music for the LORD—they numbered 288. Young and old alike, teacher as well as student, cast lots for their duties.

In *A Joyful Sound,* Reynolds and Price refer briefly to the difference between temple and synagogue music, noting that music in the former was more "elaborate" while music in the latter was more "simple."

> In the Temple, priests and choirs chanted the psalms and portions of the Pentateuch, but in the synagogue the people shared in the musical portion of the service. Instrumental music was employed in Temple worship, while in the synagogue singing was generally unaccompanied.[15]

THE TRUMPET

The word "trumpet," as found in Psalm 150 and elsewhere in the Old Testament, deserves a closer look. In the Old Testament, two Hebrew words are translated "trumpet" in our English Bibles.

The first is *shofar,* which was a ram's horn. With its sound audible at great distances, it was well-suited to increase the noise of shouting (2 Samuel 6:15, etc.) but ill-suited to be played with harps and pipes (flutes) as accompaniment for singing. A skilled shofar player might get more than one note from his shofar if he played it like a bugle; the differences in notes depended on the tightness of the lips and position of the tongue (referred to today as 'embouchure' by trumpet players). The shofar was used in war to assemble the army, to sound the attack, to signal the cessation of the pursuit, and to announce the disbanding of the army.[16] Certain patterns of sound rather than different pitches would accomplish all this.

The priests employed shofars as they marched before the Ark of the Covenant at the siege of Jericho. The sound of rams' horns and shouting on the final day of march around that city must have been a terrifying event after six days of silence—just as the shofar sounds played in the dead of night by the 300 men of Gideon in the attack on Midian were. Those sounds that shattered the eerie quiet at Jericho signaled an impending attack and struck fear into every resident's heart excepting Rahab and her family whose day of salvation had come. The Lord said to Joshua (6:2-5 NIV):

> See, I have delivered Jericho into your hands, along with its king and its fighting men. March around the city once with all the armed men. Do this for six days. Have seven priests carry trumpets of rams' horns in front of the ark. On the seventh day, march around the city seven times, with the priests blowing the trumpets. When you hear them sound a long blast on the trumpets, have all the people give a loud shout; then the wall of the city will collapse and the people with go up, every man straight in.

Think of that sequence! First, the quiet march; second, the ear-piercing sounds of the shofars; third, the shout of the mass of people; and then, the earthquake! When God 'stages' an event, He knows how to do it!

A second Hebrew word, *chatsotserah,* is also translated 'trumpet.' In Numbers 10, God gave instructions to Moses that craftsmen should make two trumpets of hammered silver. He indicated that the purpose for which these instruments were to be fabricated was not to accompany singing, but to call the community together and to give the sign for moving the camp. When the musician blew one trumpet, only the heads of the clans of Israel were to gather at the tabernacle. When both sounded, all the people came.

At the dedication of both the first and second temples, these silver trumpets were used. We are told that Solomon did not just use two *chatsotserah* during the dedication of the first temple, but rather one hundred and twenty and that

> all the Levites who were musicians—Asaph, Heman, Jeduthun and their sons and relatives—stood on the east side of the altar, dressed in fine linen and playing cymbals, harps and lyres. They were accompanied by 120 priests sounding trumpets. The trumpeters and singers joined in unison, as with one voice, to give praise and thanks to the Lord. Accompanied by trumpets, cymbals and other instruments, they raised their voices in praise to the Lord and responded:
> > *He is good;*
> > *his love endures forever.*[17]

Similarly, when the foundation was laid for the second temple after seventy years of exile, Ezra relates the following:

> the priests in their vestments and with trumpets, and the Levites (the sons of Asaph) with cymbals, took their places to praise the Lord, as prescribed by David king of Israel. With praise and thanksgiving they sang to the Lord,
> > *He is good;*
> > *his love to Israel endures forever.*[18]

Many of the older priests and Levites and family heads, who had seen the former temple, wept aloud when they saw the foundation of this temple being laid because it would not have the glory of the first. We are told that no one could distinguish the sound of the shouts of joy from the sound of weeping because the people made so much noise. And the sound was heard far away.

At both dedications, the numbers of people were very large. At the dedication of the first temple, the writer tells us specifically that *all* the priests were present and had consecrated themselves "regardless of their divisions" (2 Chron. 5:11). Trumpets and shouting constituted the congregation's repeated responses to the praise-singing of the temple choirs. Psalm 136 is an excellent example of this antiphonal interplay between those designated as leaders in music and those designated as 'responders' who would sing a repeated refrain. It is important to note that the loud music (or noise) of the congregation did not drown out the choirs' message of praise and worship.

Clapping, Shouting, Standing

Handclapping and shouting accompanied Old Testament coronations. This we noted in the previous chapter. We found the first Old Testament reference to shouting and handclapping to be related to the celebration of the coronation of a king, (2 Kings 11:12):

> Jehoiada brought out the king's son [Joash] and put the crown on him; he presented him with a copy of the covenant and proclaimed him king. They anointed him, and the people clapped their hands and shouted, "Long live the king!"

Psalm 98 also celebrates kingship and brings together shouting (verse 4) and clapping (verse 8 which is clearly poetical). These references are not sufficient justification for a doctrine that suggests handclapping and shouting are *requirements* for worship. On the other hand, they certainly do not teach that handclapping is inappropriate in worship.

Handclapping has come about in the contemporary evangelical church, not because it is a biblical requirement that has been neglected, but because we tend to be a more emotional people who want to express our emotions—and are willing to do so publicly. When a church can no longer feel comfortable singing without standing and clapping, both become part of that church's *liturgy.* Wrong? No. But not a measure of heightened spirituality either.

Neither the Old nor the New Testament suggests that standing while singing is a more pious activity than sitting or kneeling. Israelites stood in the Temple although some seats were available at least in the Women's Court (Mark 13:41). There was no formal corporate worship there other than on special national holy days, but then there would have been insufficient seating for the multitudes who attended. They sat in the synagogues.

Once again returning to that magnificent last psalm (150), we are instructed to praise the Lord with various musical instruments. A superficial view of the psalm suggests "louder is better," but that is certainly not the intent of the psalm. Here is the psalm in its entirety:

> Praise the Lord.
> Praise God in his sanctuary,
>   praise him in his mighty heavens.
> Praise him for his acts of power;
>   praise him for his surpassing greatness.
> Praise him with the sounding of the trumpet,
>   praise him with the harp and lyre,
> Praise him with tambourine and dancing,
>   praise him with the strings and flute,
> Praise him with the clash of the cymbals,
>   praise him with resounding cymbals.
> Let everything that has breath praise the Lord.
> Praise the Lord.[19]

This is celebration, something our worship services often lack. There is a time to pull out all the stops, but that is not to suggest that louder is better or more spiritual! It also does not suggest that all worship must be loud and celebratory. There is still a necessity to be "still" before God (Psalm 46), to reflect quietly and meditate (Psalm 1), to confess sin (Psalm 51) and pray prayers of supplications as many Psalms enjoin us to do.

Worship Leaders for Temple Music

In *The Endless Song*, Osbeck summarizes the requirements for those who were to serve as music leaders in Old Testament worship. He finds ten requirements and lists the references. In brief, here is what he found:

1. Music leaders were chosen from the Levitical priesthood—
   not just anyone could serve.
2. Well-organized, they were assigned specific tasks and were
   individually appointed to their tasks.
3. They were educated and trained, teachers as well as scholars.

4. They were proficient performers (and) the word "skilled" is often used of them.
5. They were consecrated; they had clean hands and pure hearts.
6. They were models of obedience to God's Word.
7. They were set apart by wearing distinctive robes.
8. They were paid for their services (and) homes were provided for them.
9. They were treated as other religious leaders, with no discrimination.
10. They were to be mature (only those age 30 and over).[20]

Church leadership ought to study this list and carefully apply the principles. If the pastor is not qualified ("skilled") to lead in a small church where no songleader or music worship leader is available, then he needs training; this is not an option, it is a prerequisite. Levites did not lead music in the temple without training! It does not appear that seminaries understand the importance of voice lessons for future pastors who often must serve as the music leader in small churches.

If the pastor cannot serve effectively in this role, then the local church board needs to appoint a member of the congregation to lead and then see that he (or she) receives training at church expense if necessary. That is not so wild an idea as it first sounds. *Churches do not tend to grow when church music is poor.* The Old Testament teaches that the music ministry is too important an aspect of worship to fall into the hands of the untrained! When it does, the spirit of a meeting may be stifled if not killed.

There are a lot of young people who are self-taught and have a superficial knowledge of music. I will never disparage one who is self-taught, but I do feel uncomfortable with one who is self-taught *and unwilling to make himself or herself better skilled.* Few churches want a pastor who settles down in a rut, but will applaud the music worship without giving the notion of training another thought! Immature musicians who are content to remain immature lead congregations into entertainment and emotional ecstasy.

In *Dancing in the Dark,* the authors say the major portion of their work examines the interrelationships between the economy, the media, and youth entertainment in our own time. They then warn,

> For now, we can conclude that these connections are at once heir to historical patterns and challengers of them. Put another way, if the momentum holds, twentieth-century patterns of youth management might be following their success *to the point of self-obliteration.* . . How the young, and adults too, will find their bearings in the emerging system remains unknown. We can certainly expect the answer to emerge *via another struggle between the ages.* . .[21] [Italics added]

In the Old Testament, the lines were clear. The mature had responsibilities and were instructed to serve responsibly. Part of those responsibilities consisted of training the next generation—the not-yet-mature—to fill the shoes of their elders.

Spiritual, Fitting and Orderly

> *Let the word of Christ dwell in you richly as you teach*
> *and admonish one another with all wisdom, and as you*
> *sing psalms, hymns and spiritual songs with gratitude in*
> *your hearts to God.*
> St. Paul[1]

Many years ago when I served as a Minister of Music of a larger evangelical church, a Christian brother and member of the congregation said to me, "I have a neighbor I would like to invite to the services. He loves good music. If you plan a special musical program, I will be able to induce him to come, and while here, the Pastor can 'hit' him with the Gospel." A couple of things troubled me about that request.

First, the phrase 'good music.' The unbeliever does not define 'good' as does the believer. Second, an unbeliever's heart should be prepared before coming to church or the pastor's brief remarks—evangelistic though they might be—will fall on deaf ears. What constitutes 'good music'? The New Testament has some clear direction.

Early Use

The New Testament records the singing of a hymn by an untrained choir even before Pentecost, the day the Church was born. This group sang at the conclusion of Jesus' last passover. Matthew says, "When they had sung a hymn, they went out to the Mount of Olives" (26:30 NIV). We can presume that singing was a matter of tradition.

When Paul and Silas were imprisoned in Philippi (Acts 16), the New Testament records an instance of powerful singing:

> About midnight Paul and Silas were praying and singing hymns to God, and the other prisoners were listening to them. Suddenly there was such a violent earthquake that the foundations of the prison were shaken. At once all the prison

doors flew open, and everybody's chains came loose.[2]

Recorded in some detail in the New Testament are the songs of Mary and Zechariah, both found in Luke's Gospel, chapter 1. The former is now referred to as the *Magnificat,* while the latter is called *Benedictus.* The song of Simeon, found in Luke 2, and now known as the *Nunc Dimittis,* is included today in the service of Compline in the Roman Catholic Church, in Evensong in the Anglican Service, and in the Lutheran Communion Service.[3]

There are other portions of the New Testament that seem to have been parts of hymns as well, such as Ephesians 5:14 and I Timothy 3:16. F. F. Bruce suggests that several of the poetical passages in the book of Revelation may have been part of hymns used in Christian worship.[4]

St. Paul's Directives

The Apostle Paul speaks to the issue of church music in two passages, and we will look at these passages more closely.

EPHESIANS 5:18-21 (KJV)

And be not drunk with wine, wherein is excess [dissipation];
   but be filled with the Spirit:
speaking to yourselves in psalms and hymns and spiritual songs,
singing and
making melody in your heart to the Lord;
giving thanks always for all things unto God
   and the Father in the name of our Lord Jesus Christ;
submitting yourselves one to another in the fear of God.

The quotation is from the King James Version which uses the "-ing" or participle form of the verbs as does the New Testament Greek. The New International Version breaks Paul's long sentence into several short ones, changing the participles to imperatives: *"Speak. . . Sing and make music. . . Submit. . ."*

Those skilled in Greek feel the participles have the force of imperatives[5], but the use of the imperative form in some of the newer translations hides a theological implication that Paul surely intended to convey in making these phrases dependent clauses, subordinate to his main clause. The main clause commands us to "be filled with the Spirit." The indwelling Holy Spirit, of course, is the Source of true spirituality. The passage teaches that a believer must be willing to speak, sing, make melody, give thanks, and submit but it is the filling of the Spirit that makes it possible for him or her to do it and to do it *spiritually.*

To be spiritual, music must flow from a believer who is *repeatedly* (so the Greek verb tense[6]) *being filled with the Holy Spirit.* Each time the Spirit convicts a believer and there is confession of personal sin (1 John 1:9), that believer empties himself or herself of 'self' (that is, that prideful part of the old nature the Holy Spirit has brought to light) and as a result is filled (up) with the Spirit. And the grand result is that the believer begins to reflect the very nature of God the Father ("godly"), God the Son ("Christlike"), and God the Holy Spirit ("spiritual") in all Christian behavior including speaking, singing, making melody, giving thanks, and submitting. These are the men and women who should be worship leaders!

The Apostle Paul not only urges singing, but he says, "Speak to one another with psalms, hymns and spiritual songs."[7] If there is not music, or if the people do not know how to sing songs of praise, let there be a *speaking* of the lyrics.

COLOSSIANS 3:16 (NIV)

Let the word of Christ dwell in you richly
    as you teach and admonish one another with all wisdom
    and as you sing psalms, hymns and spiritual songs
    with gratitude in your hearts to God.

The apostle mentions *psalms, hymns and spiritual songs* in both passages. Some Bible scholars see a difference in Paul's use of these three terms, while others feel the writing device may be similar to his literary style in other places where he states a truth, then builds on that thought by piling on additional terms, some of which overlap with the original term while others contribute to emphasis. F. F. Bruce agrees with the first position and says of this passage in Ephesians:

> If we are to distinguish between the three kinds of musical composition, 'psalms' may refer to the Old Testament Psalter, which has provided a perennial source of Christian praise from the earliest times; 'hymns' may denote Christian canticles such as have been recognized in several places in the New Testament (including verse 14 above); 'spiritual songs' may be unpremeditated words sung 'in the Spirit', voicing praise and holy aspirations.[8]

Wuest on the other hand believes that "the three words are brought together here with a view to rhetorical force, and it is precarious, therefore, to build much upon the supposed differences between them."[9]

Whether the music of the early Church was slow or fast, loud or soft, unison or in harmony, we are not told. Rather, we are given a principle that says church music should flow from a heart that is "filled with the Spirit." The principle is theology while the methodology is not mandated except for the general biblical parameters of doing what is loving, what edifies, and without hypocrisy.

Specifically, the first term, *psalm*, is "a set piece of music, i.e., a sacred ode (accompanied with the voice, harp or other instrument); a psalm." The word, according to a Greek lexicon,[10] is derived from the verb *psallo* meaning "to twitch or to twang, i.e., to play on a stringed instrument (to celebrate divine worship with music and accompanying odes); make melody, sing (psalms)."

The second word, *hymn,* is apparently related to an obsolete Greek verb meaning "to celebrate" and a verb in current use meant, "to hymn, i.e., sing a religious ode; by implication, to celebrate (God) in song:—sing a hymn (praise unto)."

The third word is *song* qualified by the word *spiritual.* The noun is derived from a Greek word that has found its way into English, *ode* (pronounced *oday* in Greek). The lexicon gives us the following meaning: "a chant or 'ode' (the general term for any words sung)." *Song* suggests any kind of song so long as it is, according to the modifier, spiritual. This brings us to back to that important emphasis in Paul's teaching: *Let there be songs, but let them be spiritual!*

Congregations should expect no less out of their church musicians than they expect from their pastor. If musicians are to compose and sing *spiritual* songs, they themselves must be growing towards maturity.

What Is 'Spiritual'?

In I Corinthians 14, the Apostle Paul writes about the manner of musical performance, "I will sing with my spirit, but I will also sing with my mind."[11] The New Testament Greek reads, *"psalo to pneumati, psalo de kai to noi"* which translates literally, "I-will-sing (with/in) the spirit, I-will-sing but also (with/in) the mind." What does he mean by "with/in the spirit"? And how do chapters 12 and 14 dealing with spiritual gifts fit together with chapter 13?

The introduction of this section indicates Paul is answering an inquiry from the Corinthians and our English translations would have us believe that the inquiry centered around spiritual gifts. Note the word "gift" in 12:1 is actually in italics in Bibles that use italics to show added words. In reality, chapters 12-14 deal with *pneumatikoi*, and not *charismata* as our translations would have us believe.

The question asked by the Corinthians had to do with *pneumatikoi*, a word that may be translated "spiritual men/persons" and is so translated in the same Epistle, chapter 2, verse 15. The text reads, "Now concerning *pneumatikoi* I do not want you to be ignorant." We can safely assume their question was about the more general concept of *spirituality*, for that is how Paul answers the question (chapters 12-14). The answer naturally includes spiritual gifts.

Now if we are to understand what *spiritual music* is, then we must understand first what *spiritual* means. Here is a summary of St. Paul's definition of spirituality according to I Corinthians 12, 13, and 14:

1. To acknowledge that Jesus is Lord (12:2-3)
2. To manifest spiritual gifts, the *charismata* (12:3-31)
3. To manifest spiritual fruit (13, compare the terms used in 13: 4-8a with Galatians 5:22-23)
4. To use the gifts in proper balance for the building up of the Church (14)

Paul's summation of what the church ought to be doing when it gathers together is found in 1 Corinthians, "But everything should be done in a fitting and orderly way" (14:40 NIV).

What does *fitting* mean? The King James version uses the word 'decently' in this passage, Today's English Version ("Good News") uses 'proper,' NIV uses 'fitting' and NAS uses 'properly.' The word is *euschemon*—made up of *eu*, 'well' or 'good' as in 'eulogy,' which means literally 'a good word' or 'a word spoken well,' and *schema*—meaning 'fashion, figure,' with the fuller lexicon meaning stated thus, "comprising everything in a person which strikes the senses, the figure, bearing, discourse, actions, manner of life, etc." Paul does not use the Greek word *morphe* here, meaning 'form' ('what is intrinsic and essential'), but a word which relates more to "the outward and accidental" (so the lexicon).

Since our standard is Jesus Christ, then whatever 'fits' does so because it meets the standard of who He is and what He has done. That which is loving, kind, and gracious, as He is loving, kind and gracious, is the external representation of the *morphe* as found in Christ. It is a lie to claim that a clay image was made from a particular mold when examination shows it does not fit. Any Christian who maintains that, "We have our music, they have theirs; if they don't like ours, that's too bad for them!" violates this *euschemon* exhortation.

Some churches refer to their music department as "the war department" which means that musical skill as required by King David is not complemented by a spirituality that manifests itself in the 'fit' and 'orderliness' called for by the Apostle Paul. Unfortunately, it is easy for both musicians and congregations to confuse the idea of natural talent, professionalism, and "feeling good" with the reality of "spiritual songs."

Beginning in 14:26, Paul makes a strong appeal for *orderliness* in public services. He does this by giving very specific directives.

First, Paul regulates the number of prophetic speakers with an admonition to a prophet who is in the process of speaking. He is to "hush!"[12] if another prophet has received a message from the Lord and is desirous of speaking. If two were to speak simultaneously, confusion would result and God would not be in it for He is not the author of confusion.

Second, Paul regulates the number of those speaking in tongues, "two—or at most three," and commands a speaker to "hush!" if there is no interpreter.

Third, he regulates disorder among women for they are also commanded to "hush!" in public services and direct their questions to their husbands at home.[13] The same Greek word is used here as in the two former directives. The behavior of the women in public worship is not described, but the implication is two-fold. Either they talked out-loud to their husbands during the meeting, or they challenged male speakers in their open-forum style meeting. Either would have been viewed as inappropriate.

Losing control of oneself in a public meeting whether through the exercise of a spiritual gift (such as tongues or the 'holy laugh') or by listening to hard-driving music is contrary to the spirit of this exhortation.

What does all this have to do with church music? Paul, referring to public worship, says in that summary statement, "*Everything* should be done in a fitting and orderly way."[14] This, then, would include singing and instrumental playing as well as praying, manifestation of spiritual gifts, and the behavior of all present for worship.

Instrumentation

The New Testament exhorts us to praise the Lord with singing but speaks little of musical instrumentation except for Paul's references in I Corinthians 14 and John's description of heaven in the book of Revelation. Paul does not refer to instrumental accompaniment for singing, but what he says has relevance:

> Even in the case of lifeless things that make sounds, such as the flute or harp, how will anyone know what tune is being played unless there is a distinction in the notes? Again, if the trumpet does not sound a clear call, who will get ready for battle? So it is with you. Unless you speak intelligible words with your tongue, how will anyone know what you are saying?

Different combination of sounds played on the ram's horn— much like the different balaphone and drum rhythms in contemporary West Africa—conveyed different messages: come to a celebration, mobilize for war, etc. The music apart from the words conveyed a message much like our bugle. When a bugle plays 'taps' at the graveside of a soldier in Arlington Cemetery, a powerful message is conveyed affecting listeners rationally and emotionally.

What kind of message is conveyed when the music is so loud the words are not understood? We could paraphrase Paul's last sentence like this: "Unless you sing intelligible words with your mouth, how will anyone know what you are singing?" That says something very important about any musical style—especially rock—that obscures the vocal message by loud accompaniment.

General Principles

Having reviewed the major references to music in the Old and New Testaments, here are some principles derived from this discussion:

Principle 1. The Word of God admonishes believers to sing praises to God.

1. This may be done by trained choirs or congregational singing.
2. God's people may shout, sing, chant and clap their hands in refrains of praise to the Lord according to the setting.
3. Songs are to be 'spiritual.'
4. Spiritual singing is a manifestation of the filling(s) of the Holy Spirit which is accompanied by an increasing demonstration of the fruit of the Spirit in one's life and spiritual gifts for service. And all this in a context of loving edification.
5. Songs that edify do more than set a mood or create a pleasant setting; they instruct, teach, comfort and exhort—the rational component takes precedent over the emotional component.

Principle 2. The Word of God puts its blessing on instrumental playing.

1. Instruments accompanied singing in biblical times, but the message was not obscured by the intensity of accompaniment.

2. Certain instruments were used to accompany a repeated refrain in large celebrations when the people shouted, sang or chanted—making a 'holy celebration noise' in praise of Almighty God; loud-sounding instruments were used on these occasions.
3. Certain instruments were not used, and we can assume, not viewed as suitable, for the accompaniment of singing in the Temple on feast days and lesser holidays.
4. Certain instruments were used for civil and military purposes.
5. Instrumental sounds—and we may generalize, vocalizing any Scriptural truth—must convey an unambiguous message.

Principle 3. The Bible gives little hint that musical customs in the non-believing world were of any importance. One example, that of revelry around the golden calf, tells us little except that there were singing with high volume and dancing in connection with pagan worship and revelry:[15]

> When Joshua heard the noise of the people shouting, he said to Moses, "There is the sound of war in the camp." Moses replied: "It is not the sound of victory, it is not the sound of defeat; it is the sound of singing that I hear." When Moses approached the camp and saw the calf and the dancing, his anger burned and he threw the tablets to the ground, breaking them to pieces.

Principle 4. There is no New Testament injunction against borrowing musical styles from non-believers, but there is clear teaching that the way of Christ is not, nor should it be confused with, the way of the world. Separation, distinction, difference characterize the Christian world view and therefore its music must be different in some way from that of the world. Following heathen customs is not unknown in the New Testament where Paul permits believers in Corinth to eat meat that was previously offered to idols. The believer has freedom to eat and need not ask questions, but if someone makes a point of declaring the meat was first offered to an idol before being sold in the marketplace, then the believer is to forego his freedom because of weaker brothers and sisters.

Before church leaders decide to use secular music wholesale, they will do well to see the later discussion under 'Association.'

Principle 5. There seems to be no example in the Bible of any special kind of music for evangelism, that is, for unbelievers. The Bible mandates evangelism and does not tell us how to do it. There is to be evangelism in proclaiming the word. We certainly would assume that setting evangelistic proclamation to music would not violate that mandate, but rather enhance it.

Principle 6. The attraction of the Gospel is Christ who Himself said, "But I, when I am lifted up from the earth, will draw all men to Myself."[16] We do not find Israel or the early Church approving worldly 'packaging' for the purpose of helping unbelievers to identify and feel more comfortable—a philosophy popular in the 1990's. Such packaging runs the risk of blurring the distinction between the eternal blessed Gospel message, and the deceitful, damaging message of the world.

We will add additional principles to this as we continue our study of world views and the nature of musical styles.

THERE WILL BE SINGING!

The progress of a composer's style assumes a pattern which may be determined by a variety of circumstances, such as his response to outside influences. . .

Westrup and Harrison[1]

The early church sang despite ten nasty empire-wide persecutions. Revivals, such as those among the Pietists and the Welch, were accompanied by a renewed emphasis on singing. By contrast, the funeral notices for Robert Ingersoll (1833-1899), known by Americans in his day as "the great agnostic," stated, "There will be no singing."[2]

When Pliny was governor of Bithynia, he wrote a letter to the Roman emperor Trajan expressing his puzzlement as to why Christians were being exterminated. He said in part,

> I have been trying to get all the information I could regarding them. I have even hired spies to profess to be Christians and become baptized in order that they might get into the Christian services without suspicion. Contrary to what I had supposed, I find that the Christians meet at dead of night or at early morn, that they sing a hymn to Christ as God, that they read from their own sacred writings and partake of a very simple meal consisting of bread and wine and water (the water added to the wine to dilute it in order that there might be enough for all). This is all that I can find out, except that they exhort each other to be subject to the government and to pray for all men.[3]

The early church struggled with doctrine, and the decrees of Constantine allowed the church peace and movement. As a result, church councils arrived at a consensus over what was orthodox (we call it evangelical today) and what was heresy. Later on, the church struggled with music and such issues as

Congregational hymns in the vernacular?
Congregational singing replacing choirs?
Give up the Psalter for hymns?

Give up hymns for gospel songs?
Southern Gospel, Christian rock, Christian rap. . . ?

We do not think about it today but each change ignited heated controversy in the church. Resistance of established churches to what was viewed as "new-fangled, less-than-Scriptural, not-so-spiritual methods" is not a new idea. We need to understand that the church has dealt with change in the past—lots of it—and survived!

A brief overview of the church's sacred music shows the church somehow survived both its friends and its enemies. It will do so again.

Early Church Music

During the formation of the fledgling church in the days following Pentecost, the dominating political force was Roman, the cultural influence was Hellenistic (Greek), and the religious influence was Jewish. During that first century, we would expect a stronger Jewish influence in worship practices since the early Christians identified closely with their Jewish heritage. Early church histories note that a number of the early practices reflected Jewish religious practices.[4]

At that period of time the synagogues did not use musical accompaniment, so we might assume the early churches probably did not either. Chadwick says of early church music, "It is likely enough that the first Christian chants were simply taken over from synagogue usage. This helps to explain, for example, the continued use of the untranslated Hebrew word 'Alleluia' for a chant of praise."[5]

Athens had already made its mark on the culture of the Mediterranean world by the time Christ was born, so we should expect a rather strong Greek influence on the new church, especially after the destruction of the Jewish nation by the Romans in 70 A.D. Greek philosophy, art and language continued to be the dominating cultural force during the first century and beyond.[6] The New Testament writers wrote in Greek.

Clement of Alexandria (c. 170 - c. 220), called the father of Greek theology, wrote hymns which revealed "his efforts to combine the spirit of Greek poetry with Christian theology" according to Reynolds and Price.[7] The words are available in translation, but the original music is not. Not much is known of the early church in Egypt until the time of Clement. He is the earliest Christian to describe what kind of music is appropriate for the church.

> He directs that it should not be the kind associated with erotic dance music; the melodies should avoid chromatic intervals and should be austere. Perhaps he had in mind some of the Gnostic sects among whom there would probably have been much less sense of inhibition and restraint.[8]

The ten hymns of Synesius of Cyrene (c. 375 - c. 414) show "a Semitic influence on classic Greek poetry."[9] In the light of this observation, it would seem probable the Jewish musical style in time gave way to Greek influence. A few Greek hymns have survived from the period prior to Constantine (fourth century).[10]

The church, in its attempt to counteract the Arian heresy[11] introduced antiphonal singing early in the fourth century. This singing consisted of semi-choruses—one of men, one of women and children—with the groups alternating in singing psalms and combining to sing refrains of alleluias or other short responses.[12]

In the first three centuries, there were ten major persecutions of Christians in the Roman Empire. When persecution of Christians became commonplace, *pianissimo* singing would have been appropriate for obvious reasons. When sentenced to die in the arena, Christians sang as they were led out to face the lions. Perhaps then *pianissimo* gave way to *fortissimo* as a bold statement of their faith.

In our present day, there has been harsh persecution of Christians in China and the singing in 'house churches'—themselves tucked in out of the way places—is muted of necessity. When a Chinese believer from mainland China came to the United States in the 1980's and attended an evangelical church service, she was astonished at the lusty, enthusiastic singing of believers. She had never heard hymns sung in that fashion!

For the early church, it was not until the Edict of Milan (313 A.D.) which proclaimed Christianity as the religion of the empire, that "the singing of Christians emerged as a joyful expression of their freedom."[13]

Edicts of Constantine (313 and 321 A.D.) made Christianity the state religion and church leaders were free to travel and discuss the diversities in theology and methodology relating to church polity and worship. Church councils were convened. In 367 A.D., the bishops called the Council of Laodicea into session and music was one of the topics discussed. The delegates voted to prohibit both the participation of the congregation in singing and the use of instruments in the service. They further required that only the Scriptures be used in singing. We can imagine that was a heated debate!

The singing of non-biblical texts in the Roman service was not permitted again for another six hundred years.[14] "With this restriction," Reynolds and Price note, "hymn writers were limited to the canticles and the psalms, which accounts for the absence of hymns of personal experience during this period."[15] We are not told how the various congregations received this kind of news, but we can be sure the news was not received without mixed emotions.

Other innovations in early church music during the fourth and fifth centuries included the Byzantine *troparia,* or short prayers sung between the reading of the psalms; the *kontakion,* "which consisted of a short introduction followed by eighteen to thirty stanzas of uniform structure and ending with a refrain"; the acrostic hymns having lyrics that spelled out the name of the hymn and that of the author by reading down the first letters of the stanzas; and the *canon,* a long poem of nine odes (hymns), each originally consisting of six to nine stanzas.[16]

The church officially adopted antiphonal singing during the papacy of Celestine I, 422-432 A.D. What we now call 'hymns' began to develop as well. In contrast to the irregular or asymmetrical rhythm of the psalms, these hymns were

> made up of a number of stanzas, usually eight, each stanza [containing] four lines of iambic dimeter, a popular folk-like rhythm, rather than a classical metrical form. Here is the foundation for the long meter hymn form, which became, centuries later, one of the three basic hymn forms.[17]

The Church in the Middle Ages

The music of the Catholic mass began to take form during the Middle Ages, including selections called *Kyrie eleison, Gloria in excelsis,* and *Sanctus.* Later, other musical selections were added to the mass including the *Gloria Patri* (the Lesser Doxology), the *Te Deum laudamus, the Credo, and the Agnes Dei.* By the seventh century, about the time of the papacy of Gregory I (590-604 A.D.) to whom we attribute the Gregorian chant (Roman plainsong), the congregation sang these hymns for the mass.

By the tenth century, church choirs replaced the congregation once again.[18] We can only wonder how the congregants took the news reported back to them from the church council that put congregational singing on the forbidden list. Try this on for size: "Sorry, folks, you can't sing in church anymore."

The term 'plainsong' is most commonly used for the Gregorian Chant of the Roman rite. Church musicologists continue to call chants from the Byzantine and Syrian rites simply chants rather than plainsong. This latter term came into use about the thirteenth century to distinguish the Gregorian chant from measured or metrical song.[19] We are told that the term, Gregorian chant,

> refers to a large collection of ancient monophonic melodies, preserved, and until recently widely performed, within the Roman Catholic Church. . . Pope Gregory is reputed to have compiled a cycle of chants for the church year. . . perhaps intended for universal use throughout western Christendom, but the belief that he was personally responsible for the codification of what is now known as 'Gregorian' chant is no longer seriously upheld. The old Roman repertoire appears to have spread to France during the next two hundred years. . . Pepin's son, Charlemagne (764-814) issued decrees for the promotion and protection of the chant. . . It probably reached its final form in about 850 A.D. after which it returned to Rome, and replaced the local Roman chant currently in use.[20]

Laudi spirituali, a body of religious songs of devotion and praise developed in Italy during the thirteenth and fourteenth centuries, is of special note because this collection consisted of simple melodies rather than liturgical musical forms, and the lyrics were in the vernacular. By the fifteenth century, the Gregorian chant spread all over Europe, and as might be expected, developed many variations. In time, the church began to sing vernacular melodies and texts.

History books tell us little about conflict when these various changes were introduced, but throw in a bit of human nature and a lot of change—even a little change—and discussions heat up, fists pound tables, voices become shrill and faces turn red! That's human nature and it is not uniquely characteristic of twentieth century Americans!

Addressing what they saw as abuse in the area of church music, the Council of Trent (1545 to 1563 A.D.) attempted to bring about reform. Meanwhile another major change appeared in secular music: the monophonic style of the chant began to give way to polyphonic music, a style in which the composer pays particular attention to the melodic value of each part.[21] Call it 'new', and we can imagine resistance and conflict.

Music professors Homer Ulrich (University of Maryland) and Paul A. Pisk (University of Texas), authors of *A History of Music and Musical Style,* tell us that *radical* change has been a regular visitor to the church over the centuries:

> More than two thousand years are involved in the history of Western music, during which time a number of radical changes in style have taken place. It is significant to note that, although differing in their scope and effect, the changes have come about at approximately equal intervals of time. A major style change has been followed by a less far-reaching change after about 150 years, and after an equal interval of approximately 150 years another major change has occurred. This regular sequence has taken place several times in the past ten or eleven centuries.[22]

The Reformation

The clergy dominated church music at the time of Martin Luther (1483-1546), while the faithful served as spectators. Reynolds and Price call Martin Luther "the first evangelical hymn writer."[23] Luther produced a small repertoire of hymns (approximately thirty-seven) and affected the church profoundly in the field of music as well as theology. In contrast to the small number of hymns Luther wrote, Charles Wesley and Fanny Crosby each produced hymns in the thousands.[24]

Luther's hymns were full of strength and courage, but more than that, they were in the vernacular, the people's language. He departed from tradition and encouraged congregational singing. Luther wrote to a pastor at Zwickau during the reformation wishing

> that we had as many songs as possible in the vernacular which the people could sing during mass. . .[25]

Luther's plea did not go unheard. Koch in his work, *Geschichte des Kirchenlieds und Kirchengesanges,* counted fifty-one hymn-writers actively composing during the years 1517 to 1560. A note that appeared in the preface of a 1546 hymnal (the year of Luther's death) reads as follows:

> Throughout half of Germany there is scarcely a pastor or shoemaker who lacks the skill to make a little song or tune to sing at church with his neighbors.[26]

This sounds very modern! Today we have no lack of the simplest of folk writing hymns and songs to be sung in the churches. To assume that only the well-trained can compose a hymn of praise to God is snobbery. To assume that the untrained have a corner on producing worthy or worshipful church music is equal snobbery. Worship does not depend on skill or simplicity though each can contribute to it. It is primarily a matter of the heart (not emotions, but spiritual maturing).

Both the "Hallelujah Chorus" from a skilled composer such as Handel, and the very simple, anonymous "American Melody" to which we commonly sing "Amazing Grace,"[27] have equally stood the test of time because believers easily identify with the truth and feelings expressed in both selections, even though one might be called "skillful" while the other can be called "simple." The words in each case are beautifully carried by their melodies.

Luther and his fellow reformers drew on four sources for their texts and tunes, say Reynolds and Price:[28] (1) the liturgy of the Catholic Church, (2) pre-reformation non-liturgical vernacular and macaronic hymns,[29] (3) secular folk song, and (4) works of original creativity. Luther secured the services of skillful musicians to plan the Lutheran hymnody and he himself supervised the selection of hymns and tunes for the various hymnals that were eventually published. Westrup and Harrison summarize the 16th century Lutheran hymnody in much the same way as Reynolds and Price.[30]

We learn from the writings of Luther and his colleagues that he was not only a musician and a lover of good music, but had high standards concerning the new church music developing under his watchful eye and with his blessing:

> Poets are wanting among us, or not yet known, who could compose evangelical and spiritual songs, as Paul calls them, *worthy to be used in the church of God.* . . Few are found that are written in the proper devotional style. I mention this to encourage any German poets to compose evangelical hymns for us.[31] [Italics added]

Contemporary church leadership will do well to remember Luther's words, *"worthy to be used in the church of God!"* That is a lofty and spiritual standard.

Lutheran hymnals in America in the mid- to late-eighteenth century were published in two volumes. The one was the *hymnal* containing only texts, and the other was the *chorale book* which contained tunes and was intended for organists.[32] (A "chorale" is defined as "a hymn-tune of the Lutheran church."[33])

While only one of Luther's chorale melodies can be traced to a secular source, the melody itself has an interesting history. Luther allowed it to be used in one early collection of hymns, then withdrew it in a subsequent collection and used an original tune for the same lyrics. Later still, Luther's successors included the tune once again in a collection of hymns.[34] Luther was very concerned about secular associations. Harrell summarizes Luther's treatment of the secular as follows:

> Although there was much popular music available to him, from drinking songs and dance tunes to religious folk songs and carols, Luther chose only those tunes which would best lend themselves to sacred themes and avoided the vulgar, "rollicking drinking songs" and dance tunes.

> No material which Luther used for a chorale remained unchanged except in one case. Rather, "he carefully tested. . . the melodies he considered, and when necessary molded them into suitability. . . Alterations were freely made."[35]

Luther sharply warned against indiscriminate use of secular sources. He wrote in a letter to George Spalatin, chaplain for Elector Frederick of Saxony, that "any new words or the language used at court" ought to be avoided in favor of "the most common words" that give evidence of being "pure and apt."[36] Luther did not have a very favorable impression of conversations at the Elector's court!

Drinking songs and dance music were entirely too rhythmical for Luther so he recommended de-rhythmizing them to negate worldly influence. He also attempted to strengthen the spiritual influence of his hymnody by using Scripture and allusions to Scripture in the texts.[37] Admittedly, few church leaders today would have the expertise of a Luther to alter contemporary songs, but there is a need to effect some "spiritual influence" by teaching musicians to be selective since there is such a large repertoire available.

Ulrich Zwingli (1484-1531), a Swiss priest, was strongly opposed to certain Roman Catholic teachings on the grounds they interfered with personal freedom. His theology and concept of church music "differed widely" from that of Luther.[38] Ulrich and Pisk tell us that

> adherents of Zwingli forcibly removed art works from the churches, destroyed organs and other instruments, and virtually abandoned music, feeling that music reflected the Catholic tradition.[39]

John Calvin (1509-1564), a French theologian, developed a message of reform and austerity. Eventually the local government of Geneva, Switzerland, came under his influence. He exerted strong influence on church music in the sixteenth century. He had many "firm convictions" including the conviction that congregational singing was to be limited to singing the versified psalms in the vernacular. He would not permit the use of hymns, including those of Luther and his associates, although he did permit the singing of some Psalms to Lutheran melodies.[40] Singing was generally in unison without accompaniment.[41] Calvin promoted simplicity and modesty in church music.

One can easily believe that Calvin's personality was strong and persuasive to set such a standard in the emotional mine-field of music, yet he continued to command a large following.

The *Genevan Psalter* was published in 1562, and in that year there were more than twenty-five editions, followed then by eighty additional editions in the next thirty-eight years. In the seventeenth century, ninety more editions appeared. Probably no other publication has influenced western hymnody as much as the *Genevan Psalter*. Only a few psalms in metrical or versified form from the old Psalters survived and may be found in modern hymnals. One that has survived, Psalm 23, appeared first in *The Scottish Psalter* (A.D. 1650):

> The Lord's my shepherd, I'll not want; He makes me down to lie.
> In pastures green, He leadeth me The quiet waters by.
>
> My soul He doth restore again, And me to walk doth make
> Within the paths of righteousness, Even for His own name's sake.
>
> Yea, though I walk through death's dark vale, Yet will I fear no ill;
> For Thou are with me, and Thy rod And staff me comfort still.
>
> My table Thou hast furnished In presence of my foes;
> My head Thou dost with oil anoint, And my cup overflows.
>
> Goodness and mercy all my life Shall surely follow me;
> And in God's house forevermore My dwelling place shall be.

Monophony, the characteristic style of church music through-out much of the Middle Ages, gave way to polyphony (the first true examples are found in the eleventh and twelfth centuries). In turn, this style gave way to still another change, homophony,[42] a style with which we are most familiar though we may not know its name. In this style, the melody is found in one part or another (generally in the soprano) and harmonized by other parts in the form of chords. Luther's chorales as well as subsequent hymns are written in this style. Contemporary hymnals contain tunes of this style almost exclusively.

Before Lukas Osiander's hymnal was published in Nürnberg in

1586, church musicians were composing for both choir and congregation. His hymnal, *Fifty Spiritual Songs and Psalms,* was homophonic in musical style.[43] Osiander's additional contribution to the church music of his day was a hymnal written in such a way that both choirs and congregations could use it, surely a change that must have pleased many!

The Pietist movement, beginning with Jakob Spener about 1670, had considerable influence on church hymnody. The movement emphasized a subjective religious thought pattern and Pietist hymns had an intense personal quality with singular pronouns replacing plural ones, that is, 'I' replacing the plural 'we'. Such poems did not fit the old chorale-type tunes. The more personal and passionate quality of religious experience required new musical accompaniments.

There will be singing! Let's pray it will be *spiritual* whatever the style.

In the next chapter we shall examine several musical styles adopted by the church over the last three hundred years. It is sufficient to note at this point that music in the church has not been static. Change suggests stress, but the church has been enriched through its broadening repertoire of musical styles.

. . . And More Singing!

O for a thousand tongues to sing
My great Redeemer's praise,
The glories of my God and King,
The triumphs of His grace!

Charles Wesley

How do we get others to remember what we feel is important for them to remember? The answer is quite simple. My children learned their ABCs more quickly because my wife and I taught them using an alphabet song. How do I remember the order of the books of the Bible? Simple. At a Vacation Bible School when I was a child someone taught us a song using the names of the books of the Bible. After Daniel and before Malachi, I still let the tune help me find one of the minor prophets! And who uses this little 'trick' to great advantage? Advertisers. Set a client's product to a catchy jingle, and profits begin to roll in.

Just so in the eighteenth century. It was then that many English clergymen began to compose hymns filled with generous doses of doctrine rather than the worshipful concepts of the psalms. Pastors often wrote hymns to accompany their sermons and in this way helped believers, many of whom were illiterate, to remember the truth taught in the Sunday sermons. Singing reinforced the doctrinal message of the sermon throughout the week.

Hymn Musical Style

In the early eighteenth century, the church in Europe once again witnessed a decline in congregational singing and a resurgence of choir-singing. There was a growing prominence of the solo and accompanying organ, thanks to the marvelous talent of Johann Sebastian Bach (1685-1750) who did little to encourage congregational singing. He wrote a large magnificent repertoire of music for choirs which provided all the music for worship. A generation after Bach, this "concert style of music was banished from the service."[1]

At first, hymns were poems written about God and human religious experiences and were not initially set to music. In time, a few hymns found their way into some of the Psalter editions. Reynolds and Price report that in the latter part of the seventeenth century, Psalters were already on the wane with hymn-singing beginning to gain ground in popularity.[2]

The hymn style eventually achieved a legitimate place in church worship but, as we might have guessed, only after conflict. Hymn lyrics were objective, didactic and utilitarian in form. Not surprisingly, there were those who viewed the hymn as inferior to the metrical psalm for the hymn was *about* Scripture rather than Scripture itself. The Psalter through usage and acceptance had come to be viewed as "inspired."

An example of the hymn style, "O Worship the King," written by Robert Grant (circa 1779-1833), illustrates how the hymn served to reinforce the theology of the nature of God. In the following three stanzas, note how much is said about who God is:

O worship the King, all glorious above;
Oh gratefully sing His power and His love;
Our Shield and Defender, the Ancient of Days,
Pavilioned in splendor, and girded with praise.

Oh, tell of His might, Oh, sing of His grace,
Whose robe is the light, whose canopy space;
His chariots of wrath the deep thunder-clouds form,
And dark is His path on the wings of the storm.

Frail children of dust, and feeble as frail,
In Thee do we trust, nor find Thee to fail:
Thy mercies how tender, how firm to the end,
Our Maker, Defender, Redeemer, and Friend.

Many eighteenth century hymns survived and enjoy a place in our hymnals. There is strength both in the words and music. They have met the test of "literary quality and music worthy of the tune," to quote Reynolds and Price.[3]

Because the singing of hymns involves a musical experience, it is imperative that attention be given to the intrinsic musical values of the hymn tune. *Great literary expressions cannot*

have fullest meaning when coupled with inferior tunes.
Because of their contribution, the appropriateness of text,
melody, harmony, and rhythm requires critical examination.
From a musical standpoint this is not to imply that complex
and intricate tunes are the ideal, for hymn tunes are the people's songs. But it does stress the fact that the literary quality
of the hymn *and the music worthy of the tune* merit careful
study and thoughtful appraisal. [Italics added]

The stage is now set for Isaac Watts and John and Charles
Wesley. Isaac Watts (1674-1748) contributed immensely to the new
hymn repertoire, but his philosophy of church music and that of
John Calvin differed considerably. Watts believed the church should
sing freely composed hymns which reflected the experiences of
those who wrote them.

Watts, the father of English hymnody, wrote hymns "based on
the experiences, thoughts, and aspirations common to all Christians
expressed in what might be called classic objectivity."[4] With few
exceptions his 350 hymns were set to the three simplest metrical
forms of music: long, short, and common.[5] This type of hymn organization (the meter is the number of syllables per line) is generally
found at the beginning of a hymn and was a change from earlier
chants that were free form.

Comparing the psalter-style Twenty-third Psalm to a nineteenth
century hymn written by Henry W. Baker (1821-1877), we discover
immediately that the hymn form, though more structured in terms of
the tune, has more lyrical flexibility and the words flow more freely.

> The King of love my shepherd is, Whose goodness faileth never;
> I nothing lack if I am His And He is mine forever.
>
> Where streams of living water flow My ransomed soul He leadeth,
> And where the verdant pastures grow, With food celestial feedeth.
>
> Perverse and foolish oft I strayed; But yet in love He sought me,
> And on His shoulder gently laid, And home, rejoicing, brought me.
>
> In death's dark vale I fear no ill With Thee, dear Lord, beside me;
> Thy rod and staff my comfort still, Thy cross before to guide me.
>
> Thou spreadst a table in my sight; Thy unction grace bestoweth;
> And, oh, what transport of delight From Thy pure chalice floweth.

And so through all the length of days Thy goodness faileth never:
Good Shepherd, may I sing Thy praise Within Thy house forever.

In 1741, John Wesley (1703-1791) published his first collection of 152 hymns in London. Since he disliked the old psalm tunes, he published a collection of hymns with new tunes. This collection gained notoriety as being "one of the worst printed books ever issued"[6] due to bad printing and a multitude of mistakes.

Almost all Wesleyan hymn-singing was without instrumental accompaniment because any accompaniment in Wesley's large outdoor meetings lacking public address systems would have been drowned out. According to Curwen, only three of Wesley's chapels ever introduced organs into their services.[7]

An excerpt from the *Minutes of Conference,* 1768, deals with Wesley's concern about formality and repetition:

> Beware of formality in singing, or it will creep upon us unawares. "Is it not creeping in already," said they, "by these complex tunes which it is scarcely possible to sing with devotion?" Such is "Praise the Lord, ye blessed ones"; such the long quavering hallelujah annexed to the morning song tune, which I defy any man living to sing devoutly. The repeating the same so often, as it shocks all common sense, so it necessarily brings in dead formality, and has no more religion in it than a Lancashire hornpipe. Besides that, it is a flat contradiction to our Lord's command, "Use not vain repetitions." For what is vain repetition, if this is not? What end of devotion does it serve? Again, do not suffer the people to sing too slow. This naturally tends to formality, and is brought in by those who have strong or very weak voices. Is it not possible that all the Methodists in the nation should sing equally quick?

Singing with much repetition is a practice being revived by the charismatic tradition. We are not told why the practice developed in England, but we can be sure Wesley saw it as unspiritual.

In the late eighteenth century, trivial tunes became widely used and the popular, excessively florid style, according to some musicologists "greatly weakened the strength of Methodist hymn-singing as the nineteenth century approached."[8] This style was heavily influenced by changes occurring in the secular society, changes which ushered in what we now call romanticism. This new style had a strong emotional content, as did the gospel song introduced towards the close of the nineteenth century, and as do the new musical styles introduced in the last half of the twentieth century.

In the nineteenth century, the philosophical, artistic and literary movements that began in the previous century, came to full flower. This romanticism was in essence a revolt against the restrictions of formalism and objectivity as found in a previous revival of old forms called neoclassicism. Historians further clarify the romantic movement in this way:

> Just because classicism sought to express the idea of beauty in definite and objective forms, it was possible to lay down fixed canons of procedure and so to render the result formal, precise and almost mechanical. Romanticism, however, aims to represent what is inner and subjective, and, therefore, necessarily protests against making art stilted and formal by the application of external rules and mechanical standards. Art, the Romanticists declare, must spring from the untrammeled expression of the free spirit of the man of genius. "The will or caprice of the poet," as Schlegel says, "admits no law above itself."[9]

Ah, does that sound familiar! What goes around comes around indeed! How much a culture has suffered by going to extremes, and how much the church has suffered by adopting those extremes!

Who says sacred music that reflects neoclassicism *and* romanticism cannot exist side-by-side? Today, many church leaders say that. For example, Rick Warren says in *Leadership* in a brief article entitled, "On a Niche Hunt,"

> When I started Saddleback [Community Church], we tried to appeal to all musical tastes. We'd go from "Bach to Rock." We'd use a hymn, then a praise chorus, then a classical number, then jazz, then easy listening, then rap. We ran the spectrum. We alienated everyone. Any radio station that tried to appeal to everyone would go broke.[10]

Warren's solution was to administer a survey, asking the question, "What radio station do you listen to?" He found that ninety-seven per cent listened to a middle-of-the-road rock station. He adds, "So we unapologetically use that style. We've driven off some potential members but we have attracted many more who relate to that sound."

Gospel Song Musical Style

A new style of church music, the gospel song, began to appear towards the end of the nineteenth century. This style was more subjective and demonstrated greater feeling and imagination and was consistent with the cultural trend.

The term *hymn* may cause confusion since evangelicals use the word in both a general as well as in a narrow sense. Generally, the term includes the songs found between the covers of a hymnal, whatever the style. We can also say correctly that a hymnal contains both hymns and gospel songs. In the narrow definition, hymn refers to the particular type of spiritual song described previously and it differs from the gospel song. The particular hymn style, the gospel song, is further explained below.

Tying the music of an age to its culture—a recurrent theme of this study—Reynolds and Price make a statement that is extremely germane for understanding why there were changes in musical style. They state, *"The desire for hymn tunes in the romantic idiom reflected the romantic movement in secular music."*[11] The gospel song musical style supplies that need. Home "praise services" and "sings" became popular as early as 1851 and encouraged the development of the gospel song which later became the primary choice of those involved in the 'evangelistic movements' (from about 1880 on).

The gospel song has been called the "most phenomenal of the developments of Christian music in the second half of the nineteenth century."[12] If for no other reason, its popularity and the proliferation of new music allowed it to qualify for such a commendation. The gospel song had its early roots not only in American folk hymnody, but also in camp-meeting collections (often ballad-style with simple language), the singing-school tune books, and the YMCA and Sunday school movements.[13] The popularity of the Moody and Sankey evangelistic team as well as that of Philip P. Bliss,[14] who teamed up with evangelist Major D. W. Whittle, further encouraged the use of gospel songs. Sankey, Bliss and Whittle all contributed to the gospel song repertoire.

Gospel songs tend to highlight God's work in the believer's life so "I" and "we" and the work of Christ on behalf of the believer are highlighted. Many gospel songs are a call to sinners to come to Christ and experience His saving grace. The words are generally simple, straightforward, and repetitious. The gospel song often has a refrain or chorus sung following each stanza.

With the growing popularity of the gospel song, conflict developed just as conflict had developed previously between hymn-lovers and psalter-lovers. When hymns were introduced, they were condemned by some as inferior to the metrical psalms. Now, it was the gospel song's turn to be condemned since gospel songs did not have the doctrinal content of hymns. Some Protestant denominations rejected gospel songs altogether as sentimental, repetitious, and lacking in depth. Despite this, gospel songs generally well outnumber hymns in evangelical church hymnals. "There Is Power in the Blood" is an excellent example of the gospel song musical style.

> Would you be free from your burden of sin?
>   There's pow'r in the blood, pow'r in the blood;
> Would you o'er evil the victory win?
>   There's wonderful pow'r in the blood.
>
> Would you be free from your passion and pride?
>   There's pow'r in the blood, pow'r in the blood;
> Come for a cleansing to Calvary's tide,
>   There's wonderful pow'r in the blood.
>
> REFRAIN
>
> There is pow'r, pow'r, wonder-working pow'r,
>   In the blood of the Lamb;
> There is pow'r, pow'r, wonder-working pow'r,
>   In the precious blood of the Lamb.[15]

Gospel Chorus Musical Style

In the period 1920-1950, "gospel choruses" began to appear and then proliferate. These were short, often up-tempo, easy to learn and easy to sing. Some had substance and were very moving, some were simply fun songs with a modicum of theology tucked in, and others were light to the point of being ditties. Many of these choruses were written for children and permitted hand, head or feet motions. The lyrics were not generally Scripture set to music as is often the case with choruses today.

Choruses from that era one might still hear include: "Turn Your Eyes upon Jesus" (1922), "The B-I-B-L-E," "I Will Make You Fishers of Men," "Zacchaeus," "Thank you, Lord, for Saving My Soul," "His Name Is Wonderful" (1959), etc.

Children and young people came to love these songs but adults learned to appreciate them as well. They were easy to remember and were sung in young people's services, in the more informal Sunday evening services and in cars and buses as groups of Christians traveled together. In the early 1980's on a tour of the Middle East, my group returned from Petra to Amman, Jordan, singing gospel choruses on the bus non-stop for three hours and only occasionally repeated any one chorus.

Praise Chorus Musical Style

Since the nineteen-seventies, a new repertoire of choruses has appeared. These are often referred to as 'praise choruses' or 'worship choruses' and tend to be short and simple in form, perhaps even more so than the earlier choruses, but with lyrics straight from the Scriptures. More often, they are based on the Psalms. Oft-repeated with eyes closed and hands raised, they heighten feeling and are used to encourage worship and praise of Almighty God. These newer choruses range from the beautiful to the trite just as gospel choruses and gospel songs did years before.

Conflict rides again! Critics question whether these songs enhance corporate worship, or whether they enhance *personal* worship by encouraging individuals to slip into his or her own private devotion. There is a place for individual worship, of course, but some question whether or not the church is encouraging private worship at the expense of corporate worship and subjectivity at the expense of substance. Is the next step Christian monasticism? That has already been proposed by some Christian writers and the use of praise choruses would well suit such a movement.

Those who sing only worship choruses based on the psalms may be open to the charge of minimizing both Christology and Pneumatology (the doctrines of Christ and the Holy Spirit).

There are some very lovely praise choruses being added to the Church's musical repertoire, including: "Ascribe to the Lord, O

Mighty Ones" by Morris Chapman and Greg Massanari,[16] "Our God Reigns" by Leonard E. Smith, Jr.,[17] "You Are My Hiding Place" by Michael Ledner,[18] and "Glorify Thy Name" by Donna Adkins[19] to name a few. Churches that reject these and similar choruses of quality because "They are not in our hymnal!" or because "Charismatic churches sing them with much repetition!" impoverish their own worship.

"We only sing from the psalter," or, "We only sing hymns and not gospel songs!" or, "We only sing praise choruses and not hymns or gospel songs!" is not a victory cry of purity but rather an acknowledgment of deprivation and poverty.

Summary

Through the centuries subsequent to the days of the early Church, various types and styles of music have had their day of recognition and popularity. The historical development includes the following:

> from monophony to polyphony and then to homophony,
> from early chants to the psalter,
> from psalters to the hymn,
> from hymns to gospel songs,
> from gospel songs to gospel choruses,
> from gospel choruses to 'praise (or worship) choruses',
> from formal choir singing only to congregational singing only,
> from original tunes to borrowed folk tunes,
> and from all this to. . . ?

In the last half of the twentieth century, folk, pop, blue grass, blues, ballad, rock and now rap have influenced Christian music. Some suggest as legitimate contemporary developments: *Christian* folk, *Christian* pop, *Christian* blue grass, *Christian* blues, *Christian* ballad, *Christian* soft rock, *Christian* hard rock, *Christian* heavy metal and *Christian* rap.

Lord, where do we go from here? What "new song" shall we sing? Please help your children answer this simple question carefully and above all, to answer it spiritually.

I suggest we take the long road rather than any short cut, and review music as art and examine the connection between music and world views. In doing so, we will come to learn there is a relationship between musical styles we prefer and the way we feel about or look at the world. This will give us a larger frame of reference for developing spiritual guidelines.

Felt Life

Song has a great power and strength to move and inflame the hearts of men to invoke and praise God with a heart more vehement and ardent. One must always watch lest the song be light and frivolous; rather, it should have weight and majesty, as St. Augustine says.

Calvin[1]

If music has power to move and inflame, then it has potential to be a friend as well as an enemy. If we drive in an automobile named 'art,' we will have the gear shift labeled "forward, fast forward, and reverse." We will find no "neutral" as Rookmaaker states quite clearly,

> Art is not neutral. We can and ought to judge its content, its meaning, the quality of understanding of reality that is embodied in it. . . The totality of our humanness is always involved if we want to discuss it adequately.[2]

When Stravinsky's ballet music, "Rite of Spring," was first performed at the Théâtre des Champs-Elysées, Paris, in 1913, there resulted, we are told, "the most famous riot in musical history."[3] The piece was described as having "grinding discords and rhythms" and was "of an uncompromising ferocity." The mechanics of the music, and in particular the dissonance, reflected a major departure from traditional music. Perhaps the timing was wrong for listeners who were seeking a better life, one of peace and tranquillity, not one of discord and chaos. Stravinsky's music was saying something they did not expect and did not like. They should have listened! Stravinsky was a prophet! Look again at the year: 1913.

Richard Strauss' one act opera, "Salome," was first performed in Dresden eight years earlier (1905) and it too produced shock. For a long time thereafter, it was called scandalous wherever it was performed. The story found in the Bible is based on the beheading of John the Baptist but the music and the choreography were thought to be so sensual that its Vienna premiere was canceled by censors;

the Kaiser tried to prevent its performance in Germany; the authorities demanded certain lines be omitted in England; and in New York City it was dropped from the Metropolitan Opera's repertoire almost as soon as it was added.

Strauss's opera ran counter to the contemporary beliefs and aspirations of the day. The audiences did not like it because it did not reflect life as they saw it. It was deemed morally unacceptable. Time has shown that Strauss was also a prophet!

The world was soon to be engulfed in World War I (1914-1918), the roaring 1920s, the great stock market crash in the late 1920's, the Great Depression of the 1930s, World War II and Korea in the 1940s and Vietnam in the 1950s and 1960s. Culture tilted towards the sensual. What was a public outrage then seems to have become quite acceptable today.

Hindsight tells us the audiences in both instances were fixed on the present while somehow Strauss and Stravinsky could see a future characterized by dissonance. Was the introduction of grinding dissonance coincidental? I really do not think so.

These two artists felt something their audiences did not *yet* feel, a trait I believe consistent with skilled artists unaffected by commercialism and consumerism.

Today both "The Rite of Spring" and "Salome" are standard works in major orchestra and opera repertoires and audiences applaud these creative works, giving standing ovations to skilled musicians and conductors who perform them. Times have changed. More to the point, our feelings about life have changed.

Art and the Church

Early on, church Fathers demonstrated cordiality with the arts including paintings and icons, sculptures, music, illuminated manuscripts and architecture. Archeologists have discovered some very early churches with tile floors designed by artists. Cathedrals have been a traditional repository of great art. The organs in many European cathedrals not only play great musical compositions, but are themselves elaborate works of art.

Skilled composers and classical works come to mind when we think of church art in musical form, such as the German chorales,

Johann Sebastian Bach, Mendelssohn, Handel, and so on.

Unfortunately, the evangelical church in the earlier part of the twentieth century had little time for art. Church architecture was often nothing more than storefronts, pianos instead of organs (often out of tune), and the hymns of the church neglected in favor of gospel songs.

The evangelical church has been accused of being somewhat anti-intellectual and until recently of poor scholarship. And it has also been accused of showing only minimal appreciation for art in its various forms. Now with greater openness to feelings, the evangelical church is also more open to a wide variety of art forms including drama, ballet, and architecture.

Definition and Function

The late Suzanne Langer, formerly professor of aesthetics at Columbia University, addressed the issue of *works of art*. She tells why it is difficult to define a work of art for it

> is an expressive form created for our perception through sense or imagination, and what it expresses is human feeling. The word "feeling" must be taken here in its broadest sense, meaning *everything that can be felt*, from physical sensation, pain and comfort, excitement and repose, to the most complex emotions, intellectual tensions, or the steady feeling-tones of a conscious human life.[4]

Art is the "conscious use of skill and creative imagination, especially in the production of aesthetic products," according to a commonly held definition.[5] That will serve as a starting point, but rather than argue over definition, we will focus on the function of art. In this regard, we may say, "Art functions as symbolic language." Since music is art, it too functions as symbolic language. Church music, of course, is a sub-category of music. In speaking of symbolic language, we are saying, "This stands for that." This is true for all art forms including painting, sculpture, architecture, films, dance, music, etc.

During the early nineteen nineties, there has been a growing sentiment among evangelicals—still gathering steam—that the church's facility ought to be stripped of its religious symbols to avoid giving offense to unbelievers invited to attend services. What does the art of a church (its building and appointments) *say?* What does the absence of it *say?* If art is symbolic, what does a church building designed without windows *say?* What meaning does this (the finished design) convey?

Individuals often shake their heads in puzzlement as they view modern art forms. "This stands for *what?*" Existentialism says, "It means whatever *you* want it to mean." Since the subject of art is complex, church leaders may believe it is of little consequence to the church. That is a mistake.

Calvin Seerveld quoted in *Dancing in the Dark* says, "Art calls to our attention in capital, cursive letters, as it were, what usually flits by in reality as fine print."[6]

What does art reveal? Rose Rosengard Subotnik, writing on variations, styles and ideology in Western music says it is "ideological values" which "contribute inevitably and fundamentally to the structural definition of human utterance, *even musical utterance. . .*"[7]

Language reveals something about a culture since language is part of culture. A study of any language can provide us with clues about how the people who speak that language think and feel. So also we may expect art to tell us something about its people. Even so, there are problems in interpreting art due to:

(1) the differing social experiences of the artist and the one viewing or listening to the art form;

(2) the ambiguities that often are a part of art because tangible forms (paint, clay, musical instrumentation and notation, etc.) are used to express intangibles;

(3) the listener's or viewer's own frame of mind and particular expectations when seeing, hearing, or reading a piece of art;

(4) the difference between the artist's feelings concerning what is about to happen and an audiences' feelings towards what is happening; and

(5) an intentional play on symbols by which more than one interpretation is intended—a device that is used with paint or musical sounds as well as words.

Despite all this, people within a given culture are generally hard put to tell us exactly what their art is saying. When it comes to music, the matter is not clarified a great deal by asking, "Why do you like the new music?" Or, "What does this music communicate to you?"

The best answer we can get from most people is, "I just like it, that's all!" The authors of *Dancing in the Dark*[8] found the following responses when interviewing young people:

> "I like the sound of the voice."
> "The bass lays down a nice beat."
> "I thought their light show was fantastic."
> "I listen to this because it relaxes me."
> "It makes me feel good."

Some of these responses may have a cognitive dimension to them (appeal to the mind), but more than likely, they are affective responses (appeal to the emotions). A cognitive response would say: "I like it because. . ." and conclude the sentence with an evaluation of skill, materials used, or the art form's place in the larger scheme of things.

Art reflects what a people *think* but mostly, what they *feel*. Today, rational evaluation (along with theological doctrine or teaching) is submerged in a wash of emotions and as a result, it is almost impossible to have a 'reasonable' discussion about how art functions in a community.

Some people like a certain style because it matches their mood; some like it because it calms them down when they are 'high' or lifts them up when they are 'low.' As Calvin noted, it can make the adrenaline flow.[9]

We'll pursue the matter of the *effects* of music on behavior only incidentally since others have addressed the issue. Rather, we'll try to find out what kind of life is being 'felt' and expressed in the arts. There are two ways of doing this: examine a particular style of the art repertoire, or examine the culture and find out what values were or are important. We shall do both. If art is really 'felt life,' then as cultural values change, art forms will also change.

Change in Value Systems

Today's baby boomers and baby busters opt to act individual-ly, be spontaneous, demonstrate emotions publicly and demand equal rights. They are more affectively oriented and they shall have music wherever they go! They also have a tendency to be loners, disorganized, emotional in the negative sense, and refuse to submit to authority. Advertisers cater to boomers (born 1948-1965) and busters (born after 1965) more than to the senior generation and as a result, the values of the former have daily exposure and rein-forcement while the values of the latter are minimized and worse, scorned.

For good *and* for bad, today's changes are in the direction of the affective or emotional. We should therefore expect to find mod-ern expressions of the arts much more affective in form. The result-ing tension will generate friction between the two philosophies, one held by the older folk and the other by the younger folk. Rookmaaker comments on the cognitive and affective approaches:[10]

> Descartes, in his philosophy, said that only those things which he could understand rationally, clearly and distinctly, were real and important. Baumgarten, working from the same Enlightenment basis in the middle of the eighteenth century, wrote a book called *Aesthetics*. He dealt with those things that were not clear and distinct, those that preceded clear knowl-edge and were based on feeling, the aesthetic things, the works of art. In this way the breaking of our Western world into two cultures, the sciences and the arts, became a reality that is still with us.

Rookmaaker examined the evolution of art and came to an unsettling conclusion concerning Western Civilization in the 1800's. He says the spiritual (theological) basis for truth gave way to the rational or intellectual approach to truth.[11]

> Art in the nineteenth century expressed new approaches to reality. It showed that the old norms and values were gone, that Christian concepts had lost their hold over people's minds.

At the end of the twentieth century there is yet another major change—first a spiritual or theological base, then a rational or scientific base, and now on to an affective or emotional base. "I'm from Missouri, prove it!" is losing its appeal in favor of, "If it feels good, do it!" which suggests that each individual determines what is right, true and good simply by getting in touch with one's feelings.

A startling example in the philosophical shift from thinking to feeling—and the corresponding change in values—is extraordinarily demonstrated in the film, Star Wars (1977, reissued in 1997). I dare say most viewers at the conscious level did not catch the newly-developing message. During the exciting conclusion of the film, the new message was so graphically depicted that no one could accuse the director of any subtlety—yet so many apparently missed it!

At the climax, the hero, Luke Skywalker, dramatically yanks off his earphones and effectively cuts off all commands from Central Control [his authority]. He is now filled with thoughts from his old mentor and he follows that advice instead. He then flies one more time into the thick of battle *totally governed by his own feelings rather than depending on any appeals to his mind provided him via technology.* With only a vague blessing that the 'Force' will be with him, he enters the final battle (full of amazing sounds, images and pyrotechnics) and was spectacularly victorious. The hero's actions presaged a new and chilling message: one lives by one's feelings, and not by technology and the mind.

It is not difficult to make the connection between these new affective norms and values and the arts, whether painting, sculpture or music. In fact, we'll look at this matter in more depth in a subsequent chapter. Quentin Shultze and colleagues, for example, describe the function of rock in affective terms, "Always rock and roll is there, a steady, lively, and varied companion—reassuring, consoling, urging, exulting, defying—constantly defining, reflecting, and changing his moods and ideas."[12] Note the use of the emotionally-slanted vocabulary in their statement.

What is Music?

As noted above, any attempt at a precise or all-inclusive definition of the terms 'music' will eventually lead into a philosophical quagmire in which each one's defense is based on personal preferences.

The Adobe System Incorporated produced an interesting poster (1991) that posed the question, "What is art?" and tried to answer it with the following list of terms, most of which are affective and subjective in nature.

> Intuition
> Focus
> Insight
> Connection
> Perception
> Skill
> Impact
> Progression
> Synthesis
> Persistence

Below the list on the poster is the caption, "How you make Art" and an explanation follows, highlighting the involvement of the 'heart' (feelings) and the mind (thought world). This is applicable to music. Here is the statement:

> It's not enough to simply have talent. Or vision. Or passion. You have to put them all together. Only then are you prepared for what it takes to create. Because the creation of art invariably comes down to an encounter between two of the most power forces in nature: *the mind and the heart.* Since your work is constantly being pulled in those different directions—between what you *think* and what you *feel,* between pragmatism and idealism—it's hard to imagine both sides working toward the same goal. But that's exactly what true art requires; a combination of *intellect* and *emotion,* more powerful together than apart. . . [even though] your *mind* and *heart* may never agree on "What is art?"[13] [Italics added]

To make matters more difficult, there is neither measuring instrument nor musical principle to help us distinguish between 'art' and 'non-art' or 'music' and 'noise.'

When it comes to new musical styles, the definition which may be perfectly clear to one sub-culture or another does not necessarily translate into national consensus, evidenced in more recent times by the sides drawn over the music (non-music?) of John Cage, the music (noise?) of acid rock and heavy metal groups, the brouhaha over Robert Maplethorpe's photographic exhibit, and art galleries displaying a crucifix sealed in a container of urine or an American flag as a rug. Art or obscenity? Non-art? Anti-art? Music or non-music? Music or noise?

The sound of a galvanized tub struck with a wooden spoon is pure noise to many people. To proud parents and grandparents, the first time their three-year-old budding "musician" tries it, the sound will be sweet music of pure delight. To some, unresolved dissonance so characteristic of contemporary classical music is noise and the acid and psychedelic rock styles are pure confusion. Others think these are creative forms of music.

Some admit, though reluctantly, that opera is music rather than noise, but with the emphatic qualification, *"It's not my kind of music !"* Some say the same thing about 'blue grass' and others about 'country and western.' Some find Bach boring and painful while still others complain similarly about rock. "No, it's not exactly noise," some say, "but it isn't real music either." They are being kind. By "real" they mean, "It isn't what I'd call music!"

Works of art evoke subjective feelings, so we should not be surprised by an admission, "I like it *because I like it."* Or, "I just don't like it, that's all." Feelings figure just as prominently when it comes to painting, sculpture, poetry, architecture as they do with reference to musical styles.

All the arts have an unmistakable and generally acknowledged *subjective* dimension even though painting involves very tangible things like paint, brushes, canvas, and music involves instruments, the human voice, notes on paper, instruments, etc. The 'tools' of art are observable, describable, and quantifiable, but the subjective side of art involves creativity and the artist's skill in demonstrating accurate perceptions of, and relationships to, the 'real world.' That perception may be prophetic as well as historical.

When an artist succeeds, a viewer's or listener's response will be more a 'gut feeling' than a calculated evaluation of the tools or materials used in creating the piece.

Art as Felt Life

Suzanne Langer believed the most important factor in art is "the ideas artists want to express."[14] Ideas, she says, have an enormous range of possibilities, and she suggests that the only limitation or restriction on them is that "all [true] artistic ideas are ideas of something felt, or rather of life as felt. . ." Deriving their ideas from the culture itself, contemporary artists tell us something about life *as they have felt it*. That "something" is made tangible in an expression of art. I cannot emphasize enough the importance of this concept. Reflect on it carefully for it holds the key to understanding what art and music are all about.

What Langer says about dance can be applied to music and the other arts as well. Read the following paragraph through and then reread it a second time changing the words I have placed in italics from "dancer" to "musician," "dance" to "music," "see" to "hear," and the dance properties to music properties. Her observations are equally valid:

> Everything a *dancer* actually does serves to create what we really *see;* but what we really see is a virtual entity. The physical realities are given: place, gravity, body, muscular strength, muscular control, and secondary assets such as light, sound or things (usable objects, so-called "properties"). All these are actual. But in the *dance*, they disappear; the more perfect the *dance*, the less we see its actualities. What we see, hear, and feel are the virtual realities, the moving forces of the *dance*, the apparent centers of power and their emanations, their conflicts and resolutions, lift and decline, their rhythmic life. These are the elements of the created apparition, and are themselves not physically given, but artistically created.[15]

In answer to the question, "What does it mean to express one's idea of some inward or 'subjective' process?" Langer's answer deserves careful study if we are to make our way through what seems like uncharted murky waters. She says that expressing one's idea of some "inward or subjective process"

> means to make an outward image of this inward process, for oneself and others to see; that is, to give the *subjective events an objective symbol*. Every work of art is such an image,

whether it be a dance, a statue, a picture, a piece of music, or a work of poetry. It is *an outward showing of inward nature*, an *objective presentation of subjective reality*; and the reason that it can *symbolize* things of the inner life is that it has the same kinds of relations and elements. This is not true of the material structure; the physical materials of a dance do not have any direct similarity to the structure of emotive life; it is the created image that has elements and patterns like the life of feeling. But this image, though it is a created apparition, a pure appearance, is objective; it seems to be charged with feeling because *its form expresses the very nature of feeling*. Therefore, it is an *objectification* of subjective life, and so is every other work of art.[16] [Italics added]

Works of art are "expressive forms" and "what they express is human feeling." To use her excellent term with regard to music, music "*objectifies* the feelings of a composer, lyricist, instrumentalist or singer." She quotes a psychologist who said it directly and more concisely, "Music sounds as feelings feel."[17]

I believe it is easy to identify intuitively with this statement, a statement that, if true (and we have little reason to doubt its veracity), has immense potential in understanding why younger people, the boomers and busters, exposed to a very different world than their elders, feel different about the world about them and as a result express those feelings in different art forms, including rock. Langer adds,

An artist, then, expresses feeling, but not in the way a politician blows off steam or a baby laughs and cries. He formulates that elusive of reality that is commonly taken to be amorphous and chaotic; that is, he objectifies the subjective realm. What he expresses is, therefore, not his own actual feelings, but what he knows about human feeling. . . A work of art expresses a conception of life, emotion, inward reality.[18]

As to the matter of language, Langer suggests there is deficiency when it comes to describing structure in art, structure which she calls "subjective existence." This deficiency, she says, is remedied by the creation of works of art. "The important fact," she says, "is that what language does not readily do—present the nature and patterns of sensitive and emotional life—is done by works of art."[19] Hence the importance of art to a culture.

This suggests that boomers and busters have "patterns of sensitive and emotional life" and when language fails, art provides a sort of language to objectify and convey what they are feeling. That neither the older generation nor the traditional church understands exactly how they feel is evident from the testimony of the average church leader.

If Langer is correct, then boomers and busters will not be understood until we go beyond the objective language of lyrics (although that tells us something of value) to the subjective language of the musical style itself. Let me summarize some of Langer's valuable statements:

1. "A work of art presents feeling. . . making it visible or audible or in some way perceivable through a symbol, not inferable from a symptom."[20]
2. Works of art are to be seen and understood as projections of "felt life" (she attributes this phrase to Henry James), and are formed into "spatial, temporal, and poetic structures."
3. The arts are an attempt to express what life *feels* like. Art is an *"objectification of subjective life."*
4. Deficiencies in a spoken language to describe 'felt life' are compensated for by the creation of art.

Long before Langer's time, in a classic on architecture first published in 1881 and reprinted in 1978, Leopold Eidlitz expressed similar sentiments about art. He wrote:

> Art deals with human emotions. It depicts them and depends on them for sympathy. . . That an artist who *re*-creates nature must be capable of emotions cannot be doubted or denied, but it is equally true, that during the process of *re*-creation in art the artist must be master and not the victim of the emotions he delineates. . . Art represents the idea as manifested through human emotions by depicting the physical functions of these emotions.[21]

In *Dancing in the Dark* (1991), the authors also support this notion of 'felt life.' They express it this way:

In some mysterious way, 'that old backbeat rhythm' expresses a feel for life that sets teens' pulses racing and their feet moving. The music contains and conveys feelings and moods, a deeply affective sense of life that is best defined as a free, exuberant, and hungry vitality, one that is often but not always hormonal. That feeling is the heart of rock and roll.[22]

Few would dispute that rock, punk and rap are strongly emotional musical styles of our day. These are examples of 'art from the heart' *par excellence!* If they are a reflection of strong feelings, what are those feelings?

Since so many boomers have claimed the rock musical style as their own for over four decades, it is safe to say they identify closely with the feelings expressed by rock artists. It follows that to identify the feelings expressed by a musical form, is to uncover clues about both the feelings of the artists who created the music and the listeners—fans, if you like—who affirm, *"This is my kind of music."*

Mirroring and Reflecting

A number of sociologists and psychologists in addition to philosophers and historians also support the notion that variations (or change) in social organization are reflected in consequent variations in the arts.[23] They speak of the arts as *mirroring* or *reflecting* culture. This connection is vital if we are to assume that musical style provides clues about understanding feelings and thought patterns.

For example, Popenoe speaks of the arts as "expressive" and suggests they "mirror the central concerns of a society." Over thirty years ago, Merriam,[24] an ethnomusicologist, noted the 'reflecting ability' or 'mirroring' of social organization by music: "Music," he wrote in 1964, "is also symbolic in some ways and it reflects the organization of a society."

Editors Rissover and Birch begin part seven, "Popular Music," in their reader, *Mass Media and the Popular Arts,* with the words, "Popular music serves as a good barometer of the general concerns and emotions of its time."[25] With reference to the matter of leadership developing a philosophy of church renewal, a perfectly legitimate question to ask is this: "What are boomers and busters feeling that they desire so ardently the new musical worship styles?"

A mirror draws attention to our imperfections and blemishes but beauty products, so the sales pitch goes, will keep those flaws we behold from overwhelming us. Art too emphasizes the flaws of a society and at the same time it functions as a 'cosmetic.' Art provides a more palatable view of harsh reality by wrapping it in pleasing forms.

Art provides an emotional uplift to the downer that results from dwelling on flaws and imperfections. That is one of the strengths of art for it can provide pleasant relief, yes, even an emotional 'high' (temporary though it may be). It can also provide a way for the impotent to lash back at the flaws in society, and if that does not prove fruitful, at the society itself.

It has been reported that in some cultures, one may hire singers to come and insult an adversary, a practice one would not dare to do with speech alone. Today in our own culture, some artists make outlandish statements and produce art that the community would reject if it was not couched in an artistic form—cartoonists practice this with a vengeance! The artist walks away unscathed by appealing to the sanctity of art.

Perhaps a majority of the public may resist what the artist is saying about their feelings and even deny the message. But when artists reflect accurately what is only beginning to surface in the public's consciousness, one will hear, "Yes, that's the way I feel about it; I just hadn't thought about it quite like that." Or, "Right on! I like that!" Then the art is bought and displayed or the music is played with increasing frequency.

Confirmation

Art serves an additional important function. The more one views art or listens to music, the more one's feelings about life are *confirmed*. A public senses validity and becomes more comfortable with its feelings about change through works of art. The public's daring thoughts captured and made acceptable through the license of art, develop into full-blown behavioral changes because there is a medium that 'says' publicly it is alright to have such feelings.

There is a word of warning here from our nineteenth century writer,

Eidlitz, whom I quoted above. Let me repeat it in case you missed it:

> *The artist must be master and not the victim of the emotions he delineates.*

If we are truly moving into an age of feeling and subjectivity and away from reason and objectivity, from "I'm from Missouri, show me!" to "If it feels good, do it!" then the warning should be in large letters and posted in local churches as well as in public places. Emotion without boundaries is dangerous! So much the more so when we label (as some do in Christian circles) what is purely an emotional experience as *religious ecstasy.*

Summary

Do artists just lay awake nights dreaming up change? I have tried to show they do not. Their sensitivity—a sense that must be of necessity more acute in the artist than in the non-artist if there is to be art—allows them to detect feelings as well as monitor feelings in their culture or sub-culture. They are antennas that pick up *feeling waves and objectify them in works of art.*

We are more interested in music in this study than other artistic forms, and especially the rock musical style. In light of our discussion so far, we can postulate that rock as an expression of 'felt life,' signals a critical and radical change in societal values.

My World, My Music

*People are unique in the inner life of
the mind—what they are in their thought
world determines how they act. . .*

Schaeffer[1]

Is the rock musical style a fad—and this too will pass? Is the
music something that tickles the fancy for the moment and all
the older folk need to do is to hold their breath for a while? A
quick check of the calendar will show that holding one's breath for
four decades is somewhat of an impossibility! Fad it is not. If not a
fad, what is it all about? In *Art Needs No Justification,* Rookmaaker
clues us in,

> Modern scholars, historians, art historians, and philosophers
> (as well as artists), do more than follow trends. *They work
> from a basic outlook on life and reality.*[2] Art shows our *men-
> tality,* the way we look at things, how we approach life and
> reality.[3] [Italics added]

Art is more than feeling; it has a rational base. No one learned
that more quickly than students who came to see me when I served
as undergraduate adviser in the sociology department at the
University of Toledo a few years ago. A number of male students
started college with a great vision to "go, get out, and make a lot of
money," and the place to 'go' was the engineering department.
Engineers, they assumed, made a lot of money.

They soon found that calculus was not to their liking, so they
changed their major to art or drama. There they learned that one did
not just paint or act 'as the spirit moved them.' In fact, the first
semester they did little painting or acting. They learned all about the
philosophy of art and about paints, brushes, and palettes or facial
and body movements and diction. Finding the study of the tools of
the trade did not mean one could simply operate out of one's feelings, they switched to sociology and put pressure on me to help

them graduate since they had already been in college five years as a result of switching their major three times!

Art and the Mind

In his work, *How Should We Then Live?*, Francis Schaeffer demonstrates a connection between art and social experience, and shows that changes in art styles spring from changes in thinking within the society. Schaeffer begins his first chapter, "Ancient Rome," with these words (a partial quote is at the head of this chapter):

> There is a flow to history and culture. This flow finds its roots and has its wellspring in the thoughts of people. People are unique in the inner life of the mind—what they are in their thought world determines how they act, their value systems and their creativity. It is true of their corporate actions, such as political decisions, and it is true of their personal lives. The results of their thought world flow through their fingers or from their tongues into the external world. This is true of Michelangelo's chisel, and it is true of a dictator's sword.[4]

In his slim volume, *Art & the Bible*,[5] Schaeffer discusses three possibilities concerning the nature of art. He confesses that he espouses the third view, a view that parallels Langer's theory and is basic to our approach about the function of music in worship. Note his use of the term *world view* in the third approach. What is the nature of art? Schaeffer replies:

> The first view is the relatively recent theory of art for art's sake. This is the notion that art is just there and that is all there is to it. . . No great artist functions on the level of art for art's sake alone. . .

> The second. . . is that art is only an embodiment of a message, a vehicle for the propagation of a particular message about the world or the artist or man or whatever. . . This view reduces art to an intellectual statement and the work of art as a work of art disappears.

> The third basic notion of the nature of art—the one I think is right, the one that really produces great art and the possibility of great art—is that the artist makes a body of work and *this body of work shows his world view*. [Italics added]

Schaeffer further elaborates on this third view:

> No one, for example, who understands Michelangelo or
> Leonardo can look at their work without understanding some-
> thing of their respective world views. Nonetheless, these
> artists began by making works of art, and then their world
> views showed through the body of their work. I emphasize
> the body of an artist's work because it is impossible for any
> single painting, for example, to reflect the totality of an artist's
> view of reality.

A single painting, sculpture, film, or musical composition neither establishes a style nor clues us in on the artist's world view. As
Schaeffer cautions, only a body of work by an artist or by a group
of artists can tell us that. In this same essay, he adds another word
of caution about truth. He says that

> art may heighten the impact of the world view, in fact we can
> count on this, but it does not make something true. The truth
> of a world view presented by an artist must be judged on sep-
> arate grounds than artistic greatness.

Before continuing, it will be well for us to develop a definition
for the expression 'world view.' James Sire describes it as clearly as
anyone in his informative volume, *The Universe Next Door.* He says
world view is

> a set of presuppositions (or assumptions) which we hold (con-
> sciously or subconsciously) about the basic make-up of our world.[6]

Sire does a magnificent job describing the various world views
covering the last two hundred years of American culture. He speaks
of a theistic world view (God is Creator and Sustainer of the world—
a view held by our founding fathers and still held by evangelical
Christians) followed by a deistic world view espoused by Thomas
Jefferson and others of his time (God is Creator but man sustains the
world through his intellect and talents). The deistic world view was
followed in turn by (a) naturalism (God is not Creator nor Sustainer,
giving way to humanism, pragmatism, and scientism), (b) nihilism
(nothingness: the rational end to a world without God), (c) secular
and theological existentialism (a shift to 'being' from 'doing' and to
the subjective from the objective and factual, forming a divided field

of knowledge), and (d) Eastern mysticism and altered mind states (through drugs).

What he projects for the future should be obvious but it is very frightening! His foresees *animism*, a religious belief based on fear and still existing today in many parts of Africa.

Music and Values

Rose Rosengard Subotnik also sees the connection between music and the way people think. She says, "Music, even at its formal level is to be understood as an embodiment of specific cultural and social values."[7] She defines "ideology" as "a general philosophical orientation and a specific philosophical viewpoint. . ."[8]

In chapter 6, Subotnik speaks further of the connection between ideology, world view and musical styles. She says in the chapter entitled, "Evidence of a Critical World View in Mozart's Last Three Symphonies":

> My central hypothesis is as follows: the three [Mozart] symphonies *give musical articulation to an incipient shift in philosophical outlook*; this shift shows itself in a number of late eighteenth century works of genius, took on concrete implications with the success of the French Revolution, and marked a decisive turn in Western cultural beliefs toward what we, as post-modernists, can call a modern world view.[9] [Italics added]

Her hypothesis, echoing the thinking of both Rookmaaker and Schaeffer, is basic to this present study so let me restate it this way: "*Rock* gives musical articulation to an incipient shift in philosophical outlook." The phenomenon of the rock revolution should give us reason to believe we have been witnessing a major philosophical shift in the American world view. We will pursue this line of reasoning later in this chapter. Subotnik adds this clarification,

> Not only was this shift eventually to engender in the West the spirit of what has been variously called relativism, pluralism, or, to use Arthur Lovejoy's phrase, diversitarianism, a spirit that recognizes the diversity of values and rationales within human expression. It was also to foster the spirit of existentialism which, lacking Kant's confidence in the transcendental

> (abstract yet knowable) universality of reason, concedes the
> metaphysical *uncertainty* of any rational or meaningful foun-
> dation in the universe.[10] [Italics added]

Did humanism make a clean sweep in the seventeenth and
eighteenth centuries, wiping away all traces of deity? Not quite,
says Subotnik, although much of our Christian belief system has suffered a near catastrophe beginning in the nineteenth century and
continuing into the twentieth century.

> This idea of God retained considerable ideological power in
> Europe for several centuries after the emergence of humanism,
> as Galileo's own tragedy exemplifies. This power can be felt
> and even demonstrated metaphorically in many artistically sig-
> nificant musical structures as late as those of the late baroque
> masters, above all Bach but also, for instance, Handel.[11]

I cannot help but comment on her lofty and magnificent, but
false, hope that the "Enlightenment" has the capacity to unify a culture. Schaeffer assails this contention more than once. Subotnik's
work was published in 1991 after decades of 'enlightenment' but
civil wars continue to ravage the earth, widespread famine, earth-
quakes and pestilence (especially AIDS) continue to plague the educated and non-educated alike, and division continues between
racial, ethnic and age groups, between the sexes, and between
those married and those single! There is only one unifying principle
for the world, whether in politics, the family, or the arts, and that is
Jesus Christ by whom all things were made, and for whom all things
were made.[12]

Professor Subotnik examines the "provocative theories of art"
of Theodor W. Adorno (1903-69), an "outstanding musical scholar,
philosopher and critic" who also postulated a connection between
culture and the arts: ". . . that Western art has tended toward increasing autonomy from society; that the more autonomous the work of
art is, the more deeply it embodies the most profound social ten-
dencies of its time; and that proper analysis can decipher the social
meaning of artistic structure so as to criticize art and society simultaneously."[13] One conclusion is profound: he saw modern music as
"the surviving message of despair from the ship-wrecked."[14]

From Rationality to Chance

William Ernest Henley (1849-1903), an English poet, critic and jour-
nalist, reflects the humanistic world view. He subscribed to the god,
Intellect, but also suggested what we know to be true: man deprived of
the God of heaven is at the mercy of another god, Chance. He wrote:

> *Out of the night that covers me,*
> *Black as the pit from pole to pole,*
> *I thank whatever gods may be*
> *For my unconquerable soul.*
>
> *Under the bludgeonings of chance*
> *My head is bloody, but unbowed.*
>
> *I am the master of my fate;*
> *I am the captain of my soul.*[15]

Whether the Western world is fully aware of it or not, it is rely-
ing increasingly on chance. Gambling and lotteries have state
approval. With the adoption of this new world view which leaves
God cooling His heels at the door, we should not be surprised at the
change in the arts. The new style? 'Chance art.' From "In God we
trust," the position stoutly defended by the senior generation (and
not without hypocrisy), we are turning as a society to Lady Luck.

For some time, the composer John Cage (1912-1992) let his
developing body of art convey the feeling that the world was a capri-
cious, unpredictable world of chance. He underscored the message
in his compositions by his manner of performing them: he played
them by chance. He would throw a composition of several loose
pages on the floor and then pick up one sheet at a time in random
order to play. Sometimes he would toss a coin to decide which page
to play first. Schaeffer reports that Cage developed a machine to lead
an orchestra by chance motions so the orchestra would not know
what direction was coming next! He went to extremes:

> He drew unorthodox sonorities from the piano by preparing
> it—that is, by stuffing it with bolts, screws, wood, felt, spoons,
> clothespins, and other materials attached between the strings
> on the soundboard. At the other extreme, Cage experimented

with silences. Probably his most provocative piece is 4'33", in which the performer, seated in front of the piano, plays nothing for 4 minutes and 33 seconds.[16]

Schaeffer states plainly, "Cage's [chance] music and the world view for which it is the vehicle do not fit the universe that is."[17] No, they did not, but they surely do now. Schaeffer should have looked at Cage just as he looked at Monet. Of the Impressionists, he says,[18] "Interestingly, the artists had seen the problem before the philosophers and scientists. . . Thus there was a time when the artists were ahead of both philosophers and scientists."[19] As unconventional as Cage seems to have been, he too was a prophet! If John Cage is correct, Western Civilization is not far from the animistic pagan culture characterized by fear predicted by James Sire.[20]

Contemporary artists have sensed the culture's move towards a philosophy of chance (and its bedfellows, fear, apprehension, confusion, and horror) and are reflecting this shift in their respective works of art. Their reality is defective because the philosophic shift is not Christian-based. It is not the way the world need be, but is the way the world *will be* given the shift in thinking. Rushdoony says,

> It is an impossibility for man to deny God and still to have law and order, justice, science, anything, apart from God. The more man and society depart from God, the more they depart from all reality, the more they are caught in the net of self-contradiction and self-frustration, the more they are involved in the will to destruction and the love of death.[21]

The clash and confusion of colors, the dripping of paint helter-skelter on a canvas, the film industry's horror movies like "Friday the Thirteenth," and the cacophony of sounds labeled music are telling us about our present course and what our world will be like if the shift in thinking is allowed to run its present course.

Although it is hazardous to predict with much accuracy what is going to happen next, Cage, Henley, Strauss, Stravinsky and many others we have not mentioned in this study affirm the hypothesis that artists play a prophetic role. Musical style is more than a manipulation of the musical elements, a painting is more than canvas, paint and brushes, and poetry is more than words, rhyme, and rhythm.

Overview of Western Civilization

Let me compress history here a bit so that we may get on to examine this contemporary shift in philosophy. James Sire suggested a progression of world views as we noted above. He suggests the philosophy of naturalism is being replaced by that of existentialism, the former the basis of science and technology's rational world view (concerned with establishing truth based on value-free facts), and the latter the basis for the twentieth century counter-culture feelings-oriented world view.

I admit there are mini-cycles with regards to world views, but over the course of Western Civilization, I believe there are three major world views which I have characterized and illustrated in the chart on the following page.

The first world view became bankrupt when it declared that the source of truth was the supernatural and could only be apprehended by faith, not by human reason or intellect. From Galileo on, philosophers reacted against this position of the church and began to talk about faith and reason; eventually, they taught reason but not faith. When church leadership proclaimed not merely the superiority of supernatural truth over natural truth (true) but its *exclusivity* (false), its claim to leadership was compromised.

With this loss of leadership, the second world view gained in popularity until eventually science could proclaim that it alone could and would usher in the golden age. Its position of *exclusivity* (the only source of truth) also compromised its legitimacy, and it too began to crumble. The counter-culture saw this second position as denying another reality, emotion, and rose up to challenge it. Quickly and out of patience, the counter-culture decided to 'burn it all down' and construct a new society—although no one seemed to have any idea how to do it!

Thus, the stage was set for the third major—and contemporary—world view where self as the arbitrator of truth replaces any external leadership. Unfortunately, this world view provides no glue to hold society together and is reminiscent of the cultural setting found in Judges 21:25: "In those days Israel had no king; everyone did as he saw fit."[22] The result can be nothing but chaos out of which will arise a desperate plea for a world ruler to "bring us

MAJOR WORLD VIEWS

	FIRST PERIOD	SECOND PERIOD	THIRD PERIOD
Dominant social Institution	The Church	Science & Technology	Entertainment/Leisure
Dates	to the 17th Century	17th to circa 1950	circa 1950 to ?
Key concept	faith	reason	emotion
Motto	Believe it!	Prove it!	Feel it!
World view based on	spirituality	rationality	emotionality
Philosophy	Christian	humanism/pragmatism	existentialism
Source(s) of truth	supernatural world	natural world	either or both
Major discipline	philosophy/theology	mathematics	fitness/diet
Important relationships	relation to Creator	relation to creation	relation to self
Important issues	devotion to God	the good life	self-worth, self esteem
Important values	authority	authority	equality
	social group	social group	individual/self
	work	work	play
	organization	organization	spontaneity
A major cause of death	martyrdom	heart attacks	cancer
Role models: source	religion	secular professions	sports, movies, music
Next period change agent	Galileo	Elvis Presley, Beatles	Antichrist (?)

together" and an antichrist who will respond with signs and miracles—which is what it will take to ensure survival.

If we assume the validity of the contention found in the earlier part of this chapter that there is a strong tie between musical styles and culture, then the rock musical style itself provides us with some clues concerning this new direction. This we shall find to be true when we analyze the rock musical style.

Counter-Cultural Value System

We now turn to the counter-culture. Given the observations in the previous section, we should expect the value system of those raised in a culture dominated by science and empiricism to be quite different from a culture that finds entertainment more important than science. And we should expect these changes to be reflected in artistic expressions.

What precipitated such a major philosophic shift? The realities of the atomic bomb affected the boomers quite differently than the older generation who were generally grateful that it ended the carnage of World War II. For the boomers, it was the herald of the end of the world. It spoke to them of the utter failure of previous generations to bring peace, and cast a pall of fear and foreboding over the future. Then came the undeclared war, Vietnam. Added to that, issues of race and poverty became critical. These issues (war, race and poverty) we might note, are 'soft science' issues or interpersonal and relational issues (areas of study for sociology and psychology) rather than 'hard science' or technology issues. Science's claim that, given enough time it would solve *all* problems (a theme heard in the 1940s and 1950s), proved to be false.

Musicians became a powerful force crying out that the old order (world view) was a failure and there was need for a new one. The older generation reacted since there was more, "Tear down the old order," than there were concrete proposals as to what the new order ought to be. Little by little, however, the new order began to take shape. First it was the late Timothy Leary's view that prevailed: "Tune in, turn on, drop out."

Although much of what began to emerge in the new order seemed negative and extreme, an examination of the facts as we shall proceed to do here, indicates a set of positive values. Here is a partial list of the major old and new positive values with the extreme, negative values noted for comparison:

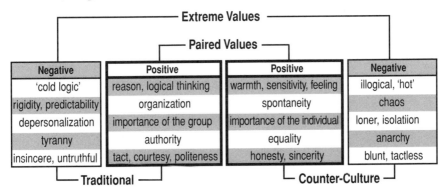

Negative	Positive	Positive	Negative
'cold logic'	reason, logical thinking	warmth, sensitivity, feeling	illogical, 'hot'
rigidity, predictability	organization	spontaneity	chaos
depersonalization	importance of the group	importance of the individual	loner, isolatiion
tyranny	authority	equality	anarchy
insincere, untruthful	tact, courtesy, politeness	honesty, sincerity	blunt, tactless

To understand the impact of the above values, first think of the positive values which should pair with each other as complementary. Who can find fault with 'authority'? No one! Who can find fault with 'equality'? No one! What then is the problem? When this pair of values is out of balance, the one positive value held *at the expense of the other*, there will eventually be a social reaction. The Church (first period) and Science and Technology (second period) both held to authority as a primary value. In time, it was discovered they held to authority *at the expense of equality.*

Seeing authority as the culprit in creating the A-bomb and ineffectual in dealing with war, poverty and racial discrimination, the counter-culture rejected authority as a tyrannical, depersonalizing force and opted for equality. Their seniors could only see anarchy in the counter-culture (the extreme of equality, or, equality *at the expense of authority*) and the fight was engaged!

We can reduce paired values to a formula. Using the Authority (A) and Equality (E) pair with the negatives Anarchy (An) and Tyranny (T), the formulas looks like this:

$$A \text{ minus } E = T \qquad E \text{ minus } A = An$$

The remaining pairs in the chart above may be illustrated in the same way. True, one does not exercise one value (e.g., authority) while at the same moment exercising the other (e.g., equality). The two values are more like a pair of train tracks with sharp curves in the road bed. With sufficient speed and enough curve, one track is more important than the other (given centrifugal force), but no one would suggest removing the other track! As the road bed curves in the other direction, the alternate rail is more important. Paired values are like this.

These values are the 'stuff' world views are made of. When the world view was basically spiritual or religious, we would expect the arts to produce a body of religious music. This we find to be true. When the society's world view became essentially rational, we find more rational type music. Now that emotionality is in vogue as the new order, we should expect the arts to reflect this world view. And so we do. The rock musical style is strongly emotional.

As noted above, social scientists have maintained there is a connection between a culture's way of thinking, feeling and behaving *and* its art. Here are some more examples:

1. Max Weber, in his essay, "The Rational and Social Foundations of Music," assumed that man does not change his nature when he turns to the arts; he expects rational man will produce "rational music."[23]

2. Simmel spoke of music that, if it is to be "great music, must embody national or social group characteristics."[24]

3. The German sociologist, Serauky (1903-1959), was more direct when he declared that sociology ought to be able to clarify the "social pre-requisites and conditions" of a music style.[25]

4. Flacks saw the role of music in the nineteen sixties as a medium of cultural or sub-cultural expression. He also suggested that "music in both its form and content was an expression of alienation, group consciousness, and revolt."[26]

Art and Morality

Certain behaviors are immoral trans-culturally, such as murder, stealing, adultery and incest, although many ways are found around these proscriptions. Some of our modern-day philosophers love to pontificate by declaring art to be above morality. We hear the claim, "This portrait of nudity is not obscene, it is art." If that does not silence the opposition, then reference is made to Michelangelo's *David* and the paintings of other acknowledged great artists. And that generally silences the opposition.

If, as Langer suggests, art is an objectification of how feelings feel, and (as Schaeffer and others declare) art is an expression of a people's world view, then we must admit that since feelings and thought life can be immoral or moral,[27] then what is expressed in or through art is either immoral or moral.

Conflict erupted in Cincinnati, Ohio, over the public exhibition of the works of contemporary artist-photographer, Robert Maplethorpe (alluded to in the previous chapter). Christians—joined by many non-Christians—saw his collection as immoral since he made human genitals the focal point in some of his photographs. This is quite different from the great masters who, when drawing attention to the human form, conveyed the idea of the body as something marvelously created by God. Maplethorpe's exhibition on the other hand left an entirely different impression.

To some, he is a true artist and there is some truth to that since he was reflecting that which now preoccupies the American mind ('soul' might be a better word). To others, because his photographs made genitalia the focal point, they were simply a public display of more of the same obscenity found under the counter in convenience stores. His 'art' titillated and pandered to man's baser instincts. "Lofty" is a word one could use to describe the art of the masters but it would not come easily to mind viewing Maplethorpe's work.

Maplethorpe's exhibit generated controversy, but should it have done that? Was he not showing what filmmakers and advertisements show these days? Respectable magazines print full-page, multicolored advertisements for men's and women's underwear with a model's stance that makes the groin the focal point. And these ads generate little controversy. Moral outrage finally boiled over in the mid-1990's, when ads about jeans à la Maplethorpe have in fact stirred up controversy and were pulled after numerous complaints.

Maplethorpe transformed what the culture was thinking into an art form and Christians along with many non-Christians suddenly woke up aghast! If anything, Robert Maplethorpe helped America see itself as it really is, and we loathed the art (or relished it depending on our morality). The reaction, however, called for the stoning of the messenger.

Is it too difficult to understand that making genitalia the focal point of a photograph or an advertisement, and walking on the American flag (as an artistic expression) are both statements? See how consistent these 'art' displays are with the suggestion that the boomer sub-culture is self-preoccupied and despises authority.

If nothing else, such art has provided us with a blunt but clear warning: *this is the way America is and without any kind of correction and renewing of the mind, it will become more so.*

Sacred and secular history both tell us that moral bankruptcy led to the Dark Ages when intellectual and spiritual pursuits were relegated to the remote desert or mountain hideaways called monasteries.

Kill the artist? Ban the art? This is not the solution. However, given the fact that art also *reinforces* behavior, a higher moral standard is of the utmost necessity. What is the problem? Let us put it right back at our own doorstep. When the Church fails in its obligation to implement the Great Commission and the *mind* is not "renewed,"[28] cultures fail.

God through a Luther and a Wesley turned their respective societies around. When there was a Moody and a Billy Sunday, saloons shut down, gambling ceased, and prostitutes left town. When the Gospel prevails, Maplethorpe's art, Cage's music, Henry Miller's novels and the "Grateful Dead" rock group will all produce a different art. . . or go out of business!

Artists with the help of the United States Supreme Court will continue to prevail in their contention that art is above law. What should scare us is not that art is free from civil control (that is commendable), but the implication that art has no rational content and is above God and morality. The Court has proved powerless to produce a clear definition of obscenity. And it will not succeed if it has rejected moral law (and it has). Despite this, many Americans *know* there is a body of material that is not appropriate for public display. One judge agreed; he said, "We can't define it, but I know what it is when I see it."

As life based on a Judeo-Christian ethic is wrung out of the American world view and as the intellectual component is minimized in favor of the emotional impact of art, it is safe to predict that the new world will eventually welcome art expressions for public viewing similar to that of certain Ecuadorian tribes whose replicas of ancient sculptures are exhibited (and are for sale) in art galleries in Quito, Ecuador.[29] These small statues molded in clay show two, three and even four men standing in a homosexual act. As the American society becomes more blatantly bold about sin, art galleries and libraries will put Adult Bookstores out of business.

The artists have been heralding in their art the arrival of such an extreme for some time. They have tapped into our minds and objectified our thoughts as well as our feelings. Their present is our future.

In a chapter entitled, "The Bases of Art History," the authors of *Gardner's Art Through the Ages (Volume II),* speak to the issue about as straightforward as anyone could possibility ask.

> The time in which a work of art was made has everything to do with the way it looks—with, in one key term, its *style.* In other words, the style of a work is a function of its historical period. . . The work of art is an object as well as a historical event.[30]

From Wholeness to Fragmentation and Distortion

Francis Schaeffer in his work, *How Should We Then Live?* details changes in painting styles occurring from Rembrandt to Picasso, especially with reference to the treatment of the human body. He saw these changes paralleling western culture's slip from a biblical world view (Sire's *Theism*) to a secular, humanistic one (Sire's *Naturalism, Nihilism and Existentialism*). He believed Western Civilization's world views, whether God-centered (Christian) or man-centered (humanism), are undeniably demonstrated in their works of art and he makes a strong case for a link between world views and art when he says, "In great art the technique fits the world view being presented. . .[31]

He asserts that after the philosophers lost their hope of a unity to knowledge—and put God out of the equation—the arts became "the vehicle for modern man's view of the fragmentation of truth and life."[32] Nietzsche (1844-1900) proclaimed the 'death of God' and foretold the 'death of man' (the absurdity of man and all things). In the arts, reality became a dream world, people were made to look less like people, the meaning of a picture or a piece of music was whatever the viewer or listener wanted it to be. The arts began to reflect the new world view: subjective, distorted and fragmented.

Schaeffer points out that Rembrandt painted the human body in its wholeness, without distortion and free of grotesqueness. Although "flaws" were evident in the artist's life, Schaeffer says, Rembrandt was a true Christian and his paintings are "the clearest example of the effects of the Reformation culture on painting."[33] And, we might add, a reflection of a renewed mind. This body of art is a clear indication of the Christian world view. Schaeffer further maintains that Rembrandt's biblical base

> enabled him to excel in painting people with psychological depth. . . [and] there was no need for him to slip into the world of illusion, as did much of the baroque painting which sprang out of the Catholic Counter-Reformation. Nature, to this Dutch Reformation artist, was a thing to be enjoyed as a creation of God.[34]

Schaeffer touches on yet another development that was evidenced in Schoenberg's music (1874-1951). Schoenberg developed the twelve-tone row. This musical system allowed "perpetual variation" but no resolution.[35] Music does not come to 'rest' either at intervals in the composition or on the final chord. The technique prevents the piece from sounding finished. Rest and completion are both missing elements. Checking with the way people think today, we find them lacking both rest and a sense of completion (which promotes satisfaction and well-being).

Modern artists, Picasso among them, became enamored with distortion and fragmentation of the human body. I do not like such art and my guess is that neither do many mature Christians. Those who do may (and do) accuse Christians of lacking education and appreciation for 'good art.' My dislike is not because this school of art lacks integrity, a charge often made by Christian believers. I can admire techniques and composition.

I believe modern paintings, splattered, disorganized or fragmented, the obscene Ecuadorian figurines, and rock and roll all have integrity because they objectify a real world-view—though an inadequate one that settles for fragmentation and distortion in hopes of side-stepping the absurdity of the nihilists.[36]

Christians are puzzled when looking at a Picasso that displays distortion. "What is Picasso trying to say?" The inability to empathize with Picasso's content does not make Christians boorish. The fact that Christians smile or even laugh a bit out of embarrassment need not suggest a lack of education or irreverence before a great master.

Mature Christians sense intuitively that such modern art (whether painting, sculpture, film, architecture or classical) *does not represent their world view.* Since one's own world view does not readily come to the surface of consciousness, Christians may be hard put to give an explanation or counter the charges made against them. Non-Christians complain with some justification that Christians need a course in art appreciation, but no educational course will change the lack of "fit" between the Christian world view and art that mirrors a secular world view.

Summary

There are six premises set forth in this chapter all of which are basic if we are to grapple with the issue of music in the church, and the rock musical style in particular. We can summarize them as follows:

1. Western Civilization was once strongly influenced by a spiritually-oriented world view (supported by supernatural revelation), only to be replaced first by a rationally-oriented world view (supported by natural revelation), and second by an emotionally-oriented world view (supported by self-revelation).
2. The revolution of the twentieth century counter-culture was a revolt against the old authoritarian order

characterized by the rational mind but was determined to be bankrupt. A new world view characterized by emotions was promoted by the purveyors of the counter-culture to fill the vacuum.

3. A culture's expression of 'felt life' not only identifies with and mirrors the feelings of the people within that culture, but is itself a reflection of the group's world view.

4. Art expressions not only reflect and mirror the world view of a culture, they also reinforce the group's behavior.

5. Artists untainted by commercialism demonstrate integrity when they mirror a culture's mores (even if believers feel their art is obscene, distorted, or fragmented).

6. Since a body of art reflects or mirrors 'felt life,' a particular art style can provide us with clues concerning the world view of the public attracted to that body of art.

Rookmaaker adds a thought consistent with the sixth premise above, *"This is important to discuss, as this music helps to form the lifestyles of those who cherish it."* He further summarizes:

> If a record is at the top of the charts (I refer to rock and pop), it means that many people listen to it. Then it becomes imperative to discuss the meaning, content and the influence it has on people—though not in the direct sense of one word or one line nor only the words. *The music in its total impact in the melody, the rhythm, the harmony, is expressive of a mentality, a way of life, a way of thinking and feeling, an approach to reality.*[37] [Italics added]

With this declaration, we proceed to "discuss the meaning, content and the influence" of the musical style over which the contemporary church is polarizing, dividing and splitting! We are now ready to look at this particular musical style, rock, which continues to dominate the airwaves in the last decade of this century. We will try to discover how it functions as art and therefore as a reflection and reinforcer of the world view of the boomers and busters.

The New Musical Style: Rock

One of the biblical words used for praise means to "play loudly upon an instrument." Music, or more specifically, praise, can then be considered one form of non-verbal communication. The music alone has a message. Again a question must be asked, "Can non-verbal messages of rebellion and immorality be coupled with repentance and holiness?" And if they are joined, what will be the effect?

K. Neill Foster[1]

"Throw those records away!" "Why?"
"Because they are rock!" "Why? What's wrong with rock?"
"That's just noise!" "It's music to me!"
"Christians don't listen to rock." "Well, I'm a Christian and I do."

This kind of approach multiplies short-term guilt and long-term resentment against parents and church leaders. Young people have laid claim to this new musical style with a vengeance and parents have tried to come to terms with it. Now the church must reckon with it. Is it art? If it is 'felt life,' what feelings does it express? Is it an expression of the new world view described in the previous chapter? Is it 'sanctifiable' and useful for the church as a vehicle for Christian truth?

Rock continues to be the chief culprit (in the view of some) in dividing a local church into factions. In fact, some churches have split over the use of it in worship services. Other churches have developed contemporary and traditional services to keep the factions apart. Is this a truly Christian answer?

In light of the previous two chapters, it is safe to say that young people feel that rock reflects the way they feel about life whereas it does not reflect the way the older folk (who reject it) feel about life. Older folk feel that since the new musical style was so closely identified with rebellion, drugs and the sexual revolution, it is not useful for the church.

Neill Foster's comments are well taken (see the heading of this chapter). He also makes a statement that this study affirms: "The music alone has a message." But what about the rebellion element? In 1970, H. R. Rookmaaker, late professor in History of Art at Amsterdam's Free University, observed the following:[2]

> Beat groups, protest singers, folk singers, these are the people forming the new art still in the making. Their protest is in their music itself as well as in the words, for anyone who thinks that this is all cheap and no more than entertainment has never used his ears.

Warnings about musical style go back as far as Plato and Aristotle. Plato understood the destructive qualities of certain kinds of music and wrote in *The New Republic*, ". . . styles of music are never disturbed without affecting the most important political institutions." Aristotle said that "emotions of any kind are produced by melody and rhythm," and that "music has the power to form character," the manner of its arrangement being so important that "the various modes may be distinguished by their effects on character. . . one, for example, working in the direction of melancholy, another of effeminacy; one encouraging abandonment, another self-control, another enthusiasm; and so on through the series."

Is there more to rock than meets the eye (or ear)? Our discussion to this point indicates there *must* be, and our discussion from this point on will show that in fact there *is*. Only with this background (as objective as we can make it given the subject) can Christians draw sensible conclusions.

Rock as an Art Form

Yes, rock is an art form even though some may wonder what art there is to Presley's music (or for that matter to Jackson Pollock's paintings or Cage's music). It is art because it is an expression of an inner self reflecting the feelings of a culture and translating those feelings into form with a degree of skill. Further, as all art does, it reinforces the world view expressed by the culture. This includes the works of Presley, the Beatles, the Beach Boys and (I stutter here and my bias shows), Kiss and the Grateful Dead.

Are these works *good* art? That must be judged on other grounds and that is beyond the scope of this study. Are they Christian? The lyrics may eliminate much of the repertoire quickly, but does art convey or reflect and reinforce Christian sentiments? It can, and that is within the scope of this study.

Definition

There is difficulty in formulating a precise, neat definition for the rock musical style even after 35-40 years but even the definition of jazz still poses problems.

Ulanov, writing in 1967 nearly 70 years after jazz originated said, "On the surface there is disorder and conflict in jazz [but] no common definition of this music has been reached."[3]

Glenn Miller, when asked what jazz was, said, "Something that you have to feel; a sensation that can be conveyed to others," while drummer Gene Krupa called it, "Complete and inspired freedom of rhythmic interpretation."[4] There is general agreement that jazz, like rock and roll, is a subjective proposition. "Fats" Waller once said of jazz, "If you gotta ask what it is, you'll never know."[5]

In passing, note that much of what Howard and Lyons say about jazz could also be said about rock. Please do not miss yet another connection between musical style and culture. Jazz, they write,

> is so thoroughly expressive and characteristic of many features of our twentieth-century life; of the restlessness, the overturning of tradition, the economic, social, and political upheavals of the last few decades. . . Added to all this is the emotional fury of the two most devastating wars that have ever been inflicted on mankind. . . *Why shouldn't the music of such times be dislocated and out of step?*[6] [Italics added]

As to rock and roll nearly 40 years after it originated, "If you gotta ask what it is, you'll never know." Since there is ambiguity, it is inevitable that to one person, rock means one thing, to another, something else. Let me offer some comments about what others say about rock:

1. In 1958, Stearns[7] described the style as, "simplified but rhythmic blues." In 1969, some eleven years later, Belz[8] identified it as a

folk music with roots in the rhythm and blues tradition expressing the feelings and frustrations of youth.

2. Rock. A type of American music that became very popular in the
   late 1950s and early 1960s in America, England and elsewhere.
   Its main distinguishing feature is a driving rhythm. . . Beginning
   as a combination of country music with blues, spirituals (gospel
   songs), folk song, and urban rhythm and blues, played largely
   on electric guitars with high, amplified sound, rock was first considered music for and by [blacks]. It was named "rock-and-roll'
   in the early 1950s by Alan Freed a disk jockey in Cleveland,
   Ohio. . ." Christine Ammer, *Harper's Dictionary of Music.*[9]

3. *Harper's Dictionary of Music* adds, "The meter is frequently 4/4
   with accents on the second and fourth beats instead of the traditional first and third beats. . . Harmonies range from the common triad of classical harmony to formerly forbidden parallel
   fourths and fifths, as well as every kind of dissonant harmonic
   progression. Whole pieces may be built up from as few as one
   or two chords.[10]

4. Writers suggest there are four important musical elements in the
   early rock and roll musical style:
   RHYTHM: "consistently accentuated tempo" (Graham)[11];
             "strict metronome accuracy" (Whannel and Hall)[12]
   DYNAMICS: "full volume" (Whannel and Hall)
   FORM[13] or STRUCTURE: unsophisticated, simplistic (see Graham)
   TIMBRE: favors percussion, guitar and electrified instruments which
             help support both the rhythm and the loud dynamics

5. In describing the simpler or earlier rock and roll, Grier lists such
   general characteristics as a steady beat, use of vocal harmony,
   repetition of words and music, simple song form, and extensive
   use of I, IV, V chords.[14]

6. My own research shows early rock (which Grier calls rock and
   roll) was most generally 120 beats per minute, a simple rhythmic
   form also used in army marches. The later Beatles' music was
   generally faster, 150-160 beats per minute.

7. In a text prepared for public school teachers, Gene Grier suggests
   a distinction between rock and roll and later rock,[15] "Rock. . .
   differs from Rock and Roll in that the [latter] is more complex,
   making use of melodies and counter melodies, lush harmonies,
   and unusual chord progression."[16]

8. "The heart of rock and roll is rhythm and beat—those twin forces which give rock its energy and propel its intentionally simple harmony and melody. . . Whatever else rock might be—and its inmost meanings are elusive and open to dispute—a concert makes it clear that rock is a dramatic participatory anthem of teen life, freighted with the intense expectation of what teens believe, feel, value, and do. Rock is at once a barometer of teen experience and the very weather they inhabit, at once the celebration of an ethos and the ethos itself." (Shultze and colleagues)[17]

9. Shultze and colleagues add, "It is true of rock—as it is of most art—that its experience contains its meaning. In the end, what attracts adolescents to rock and roll is its emotional immediacy. . . its exuberant proclamation. . . and its constant dramatization of the human quest, felt with particular urgency. . ."[18]

For many Christians, music characterized principally by *fortissimo* (loud dynamic), *ostinato* (repetition) and a driving beat, is *rock*, even though the music lacks the remaining characteristic. Some contemporary Christian music may be better called *rock-like*. Unfortunately, anything *rock-like* for many Christians is too close to the original and serves only to provoke their disdain. That is unfortunate. In fact, one young married Christian friend told me he didn't need to study the subject of rock. "Anything that makes my foot tap," he said with a degree of finality, "is of the devil." I gathered he didn't tap his foot upon hearing "Onward, Christian Soldiers" or any of the strongly rhythmical classical pieces!

Musical Elements

It is the manipulation of an art's basic elements by an artist that results in a particular artistic style. In music, the elements are melody, harmony, structure, rhythm, dynamics, and timbre to which we may add movement. The elements are manipulated in a unique way to form the rock musical style. We will examine these elements and discover some important social implications.

Rhythm

The rhythm is strong, insistent, repetitious, and supported by a strong percussion section. One might describe it as 'driving.' Its energy and drive somewhat compensate for a beat that "became drearily insistent and repetitive," as some writers described it. Interestingly, the same music that excites because of its rhythm, has a down-side: the rhythm by its repetitive nature is actually very boring. (Ever hear that word out of young people's mouths?)

Why is rhythm so important to boomers and busters? Pronounced rhythm, according to Carl Seashore who wrote extensively on the subject of the psychology of music *before the rock and roll era* (1938),

> brings on a feeling of elation which not infrequently results in a mild form of ecstasy or absentmindedness, a loss of consciousness of the environment. It excites, and it makes us insensible to the excitation, giving the feeling of being lulled.[19]

Seashore speaks of the march by way of example:

> When the march is struck up, it stimulates tension of every muscle in the body. The soldier straightens up, takes a firmer step, observes more keenly, and is all attention; but as he gets into the march, all this passes to its opposite, a state of passivity, obliviousness to environment and oblivious to effort and action. The marked time and accent of the band music swing the movements of all parts of the body into happy adjustment.[20]

The parallel to the rock musical style is all the more astonishing when the tempo of the march and rock are compared.[21] As noted earlier, the metronome beat of the march and that of the fifties' and much of the early sixties' rock and roll fell into exactly the same rhythmical category of approximately 120 beats per minutes. This perhaps explains why high school and college bands played less of the classical march repertoire à la Sousa and more of the rock variety. Beat-wise, both accomplish the same thing.

The 120 beats per minute rhythm is a category described by Sachs[22] as "the lowest form of rhythmical movement." Sachs marvels that "so elementary a pattern can be in general favor" throughout the nineteenth century. To which we may add the twentieth century as well.

Next, Seashore says, rhythm "gives a feeling of power." Pronounced rhythm in its "elementary form" (i.e., 120 beats per minute), is ideally suited to those feeling powerless because there is a perception of power in the music. He states,

> One feels as if one could lift oneself by one's bootstraps. When the pattern is once grasped, there is an assurance of ability to cope with the future.[23]

Various surveys tell us young people listen to rock and roll several hours a day. If rock and roll brings a sense of power to these young people, they will not let go of the music easily. They get 'hooked' because they cannot live with a continuing sense of powerlessness and also because the music provides them with a 'fix.'

Third, Seashore suggests rhythm gives a "feeling of freedom, luxury, and expanse." It conveys a sense of balance because it is symmetrical, and it favors perception by grouping and thereby becomes, says Seashore, "a biological principle of efficiency." He sees this principle as a condition for advance and achievement that the notions of freedom and expanse require. With the repeated cries of lack of freedom coming from the counter-culture over the years, we can suppose, then, that pronounced rhythm is a made-to-order, indispensable commodity unless and until an individual senses power (and self-worth) in some more permanent form.

Fourth, Seashore suggests that pronounced rhythm is a perpetual source of satisfaction achieved by means of the biological principle of efficiency. However, he cautions that, at the same time, the pronounced simple rhythms soon become monotonous. Given the pronounced rhythm in rock and roll, there should result some sense of satisfaction. Apparently this is the case for members of the counter-culture. On the other hand, rock and roll rhythmic patterns are simple themes of endless repetition.

Rock and roll, particularly of the "hard rock" variety, has a rhythmic twist of its own, quite different than march music. Rock stresses the normally unstressed second and fourth beats in a four-four measure (that is, four quarter notes to the measure). Normally, music in four-four time emphasizes the first beat and to some degree the third beat. Rock gives a sense of syncopation and psychologically invites one's body to move to reinforce it.

Add the constant second and fourth beat rhythmical stress to the metronome beat, the lack of contrast in *accelerando* versus *ritardando* (speeding up or slowing down), and little contrast in the dynamic element (loud versus soft), and the path to monotony lays dead ahead.

Rock and roll with its brief and endlessly repeated theme and its 'thump-thump-thump-thump' rhythms is about as welcome as a jack hammers as far as parents are concerned, yet younger people love it. What keeps youth interested in such a musical style despite its tendency to rhythmic monotony?

How is it that boomers and busters handle the simplicity of rock's rhythmic manipulation and the older generation cannot? To answer this question, one has only to turn to a dripping water faucet and the ticking of a clock. Both the ticking of the clock (except perhaps to a watch repairman) and the dripping of the water faucet are examples of periodicity without rhythmical stress (accent).

Seashore notes that we "irresistibly group uniform successions of sound, such as the ticking of the clock, into rhythmic passage."[24] He adds that this "subjective rhythm" is one of nature's "beneficent illusions." He notes that if a long series of quarter notes was played with absolute uniformity in time and stress or accent, "The listener would inevitably hear them divided into measures and would actually hear the appropriate notes accented."[25] Langer agrees with this and says,

> The obviousness of these repetitions has caused people to regard them as the essence of rhythm, which they are not. The ticking of a clock is repetitious and regular, but not in itself rhythmic; the listening ear hears rhythms in the succession of equal ticks, the human mind organizes them into a temporal form.[26]

The essence of rhythm, she concludes, "is the preparation of a new event by the ending of a previous one." Rhythmical stress is part of that preparation. We probably did not know we did all this in our minds!

The equal ticking sounds of the clock then become *tick*-tock, *tick*-tock. This organized grouping of rhythm (that is, periodicity *with stress*), Seashore says, "furnishes the backbone structure of all sports and games of grace and skill, even the humdrum of the common laborer."[27] Both Seashore and Langer agree that rhythm allows the mind to accommodate periodicity *and make it pleasurable.*

Let me push the analogy one step farther. Note the reaction of adults to the ticking of a clock versus their reaction to a dripping water faucet. Generally, the older generation accommodates the tick-tick but are annoyed by the drip-drip. Accommodation of the tick-tick results because of the process described above. As noted, the mind can "hear" the ticking as though it actually had accented beats. However, the dripping droplets of water do not become *drip*-drop, *drip*-drop. The dripping will tend to drive one a bit crazy and provide motivation to get out of one's chair and do something about it. Why?

Quite simply, I believe, adults refuse to accommodate the dripping because they do not want to, and the reason for that is also equally simple: adults pay the bill! More than likely, children accomodate the dripping. The clock, however, fills an important social role, serves a useful purpose, and its ticking costs nothing. We hear it, accommodate it, and then we no longer hear it because in accommodating it, the sound recedes into the back of our minds. A dripping water faucet has no positive social function and costs us something if we are paying the bill. We do not accommodate the sound and we therefore cannot push it into the back of our minds. It remains annoying until we silence it.

The older generation sees no redeeming social value to rock and roll and as a result, refuses to accommodate the thump-thump-thump-thump of the beat. To them, *drip-drip* and the *thump-thump* are equally without value. Younger people accommodate the thump-thump-thump-thump by according it rhythmical stress just as they do the ticking of the clock. If we apply what we have just learned, then we may theorize that to them rock reflects and in some way meets a social need. I have already suggested above some perceivable benefits: a sense of power and a degree of satisfaction, temporary though they may be.

Seashore's inventory, though fragmentary and inadequate (in his terms), is applicable to rock and roll. With this in mind, we may summarize as follows: with rhythm imposed, rock and roll is perceived to afford pleasure, for it gives a sense of balance to what seems to be an upside-down world; it gives a feeling of freedom to those who feel trapped; it gives a feeling of power to those who feel too powerless to do anything about the upside-down world; it stimulates and lulls; it provides excitement in a context of boredom; and it results in free self-expression for the pleasure of expression.[28]

Timbre

Timbre refers to the kinds of sounds used, the sound of the flute as opposed to that of the cello or the sound of the drums as opposed to that of the trombones. In rock, the percussion instruments (those that use mallets, sticks, hammers, or the electronic keyboard equivalents) are prominent as is the guitar. The electric bass guitar helps support the rhythm section. Whannel and Hall note that rock's instrumentation has been "skillfully adapted" to the beat.

Rock eliminated or reduced to subordinate positions "the flowing line instruments" (Whannel and Hall's terminology) that were so typical of jazz, including the clarinet and saxophone (woodwind instruments) and the trumpet (a brass instrument).

There is little doubt that turning up the volume on insistent rhythm with a strong percussion accompaniment conveys a sense of strength and power, and adds to the frenzy of the moment.

Dynamics

Rock and roll has been noted more for its screamers than for its moaners. Loudness has been a hallmark of the style, a fact noted by many researchers who, in effect, have raised a red danger flag because of physiological effects they believe result. A musician and audio-technician by name of Knieste who served as a choirmaster, organist, and music therapist, analyzed a Hendrix record and found it contained three times as much "noise" as Tchaikowsky's "1812 Overture."[29]

In the forward to his little book, *Rock, the Quiet Revolution,* Richard Fogerty asks an appropriate question: "How can rock'n'roll music, which is often played at painful levels to the human ear, be called the quiet revolution?"[30]

In *The World of Sound,* Albers observed that rock and roll groups using instruments which incorporate electronic amplifiers are a new threat to the hearing of young people.[31] He says that "these orchestras often generate sound levels higher than 120dB, and adds that "even relatively short exposure to such sound levels—if it occurs often—can cause permanent hearing damage."

After testing several Washington night clubs, consumer advocate Ralph Nader reported that sound readings fell between 100 and 116 decibels, and in some discotheques elsewhere they have reached to 138dB.[32] Since the danger level is 80 decibels, the threshold of pain is 120 decibels, and the lethal level is 180 decibels,[33] that assault on the eardrums is deadly to the physical well-being of those who are in close range. An anonymous wit once said, "Today, it isn't facing the music that hurts, it's listening to it."

The loud dynamic was an essential part of rock and roll for two reasons. First, it enhanced the feeling of power since sound which overwhelms produces that effect. Second, it was the best megaphone any announcer could want.

Loud, driving music provides an appearance of power and gives listeners a high-octane boost. When it is over, as others have noted, listeners are *drained*. The power is short lived. It has no persuasive power to take its audience on to self-denial or acts of selfless service. It is a momentary high followed by an inevitable compensating low, two psychological events repeated over and again in the lives of many of rock's devotees.

An admirer of rock, Janet Rotter, who wrote in *Glamour Magazine,* under the byline, "Sound," presents a more subjective view on how one listens to rock.

> One listens to Janis Joplin with one's gut, with one's spine, below the belt, in the spasm of a muscle. She shrieks "Pierce My Heart"; you contract and embrace yourself. She howls out of the meanness of a fallen woman; you say, "yeah," and you identify and you sympathize. She wails Big Mamma Thorton's "Ball and Chain," inhaling crescendos of violence into soft lullaby moans and you shudder or shiver.[34]

DeMott suggests rock sound overwhelms "separateness, the mental operations that discern and define here and there, me and not-me." DeMott continues, "Pounded by volume, riddled by light, the listener slides free from the restraining self and from the pretenses of a private, 'unique' rationality."[35]

If music has the power to erase "the mental operations that discern and define," then the result is some sort of ecstasy. Christians should be leery of anything that causes one to "slide free from the restraining self." Christians generally oppose hypnotism for this very reason. The only One Christians want to take control of them is the Spirit of God who fills, controls, and enables him or her to manifest spiritual fruit and gifts.[36]

Reich[37] speaks of rock music as "a pulsing new energy" and comments, "Not even the turbulent fury of Beethoven's Ninth Symphony can compete for sheer energy with the Rolling Stones." Energy is power and the powerless seek after any promise of power, feel of power, or illusion of power. DeMott[38] notes many seek relief from significant life quandaries and guilt, and rock gives relief; unhappily, it is like alcohol and drugs which give only temporary relief. DeMott adds,

> All are alike, though, in their relish for a thunderous, enveloping, self-shattering moment wherein the capacity for evaluating an otherness is itself rocked and shaken, and the mob of the senses cries out: "What we feel, we are!"[39]

Rock serves as a megaphone. Loud music stops everything else in its tracks. It demands attention and unless one walks out of a concert, it will have one's attention. The counter-culture demanded to be noticed and as rock musicians cranked up the sound with powerful amplifiers and giant speakers, it was noticed. Rock is a marvelous attention-grabber!

Form (Structure)

The form or structure of rock and roll as a musical style is characterized by two important departures from what most music listeners have come to view as "normal," that is, contrast and complexity. All early rock and much of later rock lack these two essential ingredients.

The basic rock and roll style (that of Presley and his imitators) was very simple in structure. Three major chords were sufficient to launch rock and roll and keep it going for a decade. It then began to develop more complex rhythms in the nineteen sixties (Graham[40]) and this made critics wonder if rock and roll was following the trend of jazz and "fast getting less danceable."[41] The

Beatles contributed to this development by introducing rock music which had a metronomic beat in the 160 beats-per-minute range, faster than the earlier rock style which remained constant around at 120.[42] Perhaps this is why their rock appealed to college students.

Various researchers note the simplicity in rock's structure in the early years. Cohn[43] flatly stated, "Rock and roll was very simple music." All that mattered, he wrote, is "the noise it makes, its drive, its aggressions, its newness." Its simplicity allowed even a novice guitar player to compose 'hits.'

Simplicity in form should not surprise us for two reasons. Young people may have knowledge (television and the educational process see to that) but not experience or wisdom; they are not yet mature adults. Dr. James Dobson and other contemporary psychologists have suggested adolescence continues to age twenty-five or twenty-eight. I have seen adolescent behavior in too many who are thirty and more. At that age, I fear it has become a way of life.

In the rock style, *fortissimo* (loudness) is not offset by *pianissimo* (softness, quietness or tranquillity); *allegro* (fast) is not offset by *andante* or *largo* (slow); there is no *accelerando* (speeding up) or *ritardando* (slowing down); and there is minimal alternation between different kinds of instruments. The musicians and the listeners seem to be content with a sameness that prompted Whannel and Hall to comment that the conditions of production of pop music very much resemble those of the assembly line.[44]

We should not fail to note that the feelings and attitudes accompanying the earlier simple yet rhythmical American music (e.g., Negro spirituals, Stephen Foster's songs, ballads, etc.) also reflected alienation, pain, and escape.

Movement

In light of Langer's views on rhythm,[45] there is some question as to whether rock and roll truly contains "musical movement." In musical movement, one senses the passage of time through musical figures (or, structures) which take the listener from points of origin to points of relative rest, from tensions to resolutions.

As noted earlier, Graham suggests that rock lacks tension because of its "consistently and oppressively emphasized" four-four beat. If there is motion to rock, it is a rocking back-and-forth motion (Point A to B to A to B to A. . .) rather than a motion that starts somewhere (Point A) and "goes" somewhere (Point B to Point C to. . .).

Classical music produces climaxes by changes in dynamics (loud contrasted with soft) and tempo (fast contrasted with slow). When a selection reaches its final resolution, a listener has experienced a sense of 'motion,' which is apparent or 'virtual' rather than actual. Its nature is psychological and emotional rather than physical or spatial.

In view of our premise, "music is what life feels like," we can now raise the following question: If rock and roll structurally presents minimal motion by starting at point A only to come back to A and start again—and again and again—does the music reflect a mind-set without goals? I firmly believe so. An examination of the counter-culture would lead us to believe that, and the philosophy of the day—existentialism—confirms this very contention. For many, goals are short-term, such as what one is going to do *tonight* or on the weekend. Too many younger people take ten to twenty years "to find themselves" and in the process work at this job a while and that job a while. It is A to B and back again, over and over again.

Modern classical music, we might note in passing, is characterized by dissonance or discord. The difference between traditional classical music (which also employs dissonance) and modern classical music, is that the former resolves dissonant chords, while the latter leaves them unresolved. Life has always been full of dissonance, but when the Judeo-Christian ethic was in evidence, there was always hope, resolution and rest. Today, boomers' and busters' existential philosophy has little patience with the past and no hope for the future.

"What are you doing tomorrow night?" "I won't know until tomorrow; call me then." "Tear down the society; it has failed,"—but no one had a blueprint for rebuilding. Neither existentialism nor rock is much interested in the progression of time, and certainly has little interest in the past or future. A rocking back-and-forth 'now' experience will do quite well, thank you.

Harmony

Harmony, as noted above, is not a strong suit in early rock and roll music although it is given a bit more prominence in the later rock of the Beatles and the Beach Boys. We need only comment here on the effect of using a bare-bones harmony structure with so few chord progressions.

Classical harmony carries the mind gently, gracefully, and peacefully from one point to the next through subtle transitions; it then returns to 'home base' with peaceful resolution. The harmonies of rock on the other hand are abrupt with the movement from one chord to another confrontively demanding, "Get out of my way!" The subtlety of chord progressions (moving from one key to another in a series of steps) is a luxury rock can do without. Rock is blunt, a reflection of speech today: blunt and confrontational. St. Paul's message to the Ephesians is forgotten: "Speak the truth *in love.*"[46]

Melody

One might think that a discussion about a musical style would begin with what is generally assumed to be the most obvious thing about music: melody. In improvisational jazz, easy listening, and most of rock, melody is not the major element as it is in other musical styles.

Why are these elements put together in such a fashion and why does the resulting rock style continue to be so popular? Grier says it well:[47]

> Young people today use rock as a means of expressing their feelings, attitudes, and philosophies, communicating not only musical but social ideas as well. . . We all know now that music is a very important mode of expression.

Rock: Do We or Don't We?

> *Everything is permissible—but not everything is beneficial. Everything is permissible—but not everything is constructive.*
>
> St. Paul[1]

S o younger people have a world view different than the seniors. So they express their feelings through the rock musical style. So rock is a form of art. So what? Do we use the rock musical style or the rock-like derivative styles in church? Is the musical style the "devil's diversion" or is it 'sanctifiable' and useful for the Master's service?

In his earlier books on rock, Bob Larson labeled it "the devil's diversion." Later, he came to this conclusion:

> Quite frankly, I saw no hope that an authentic, spiritually viable idiom of musical expression could come out of such confusion. It didn't seem possible that these gospel rock artists would ever mellow and mature into composers and singers who would explore themes of depth and commitment worthy of acceptance by the church. But in many ways, I was dead wrong![2]

Without question, the message of rock and roll (lyrics and/or music) has conveyed "rebellion and immorality." Rock songs broadsided society's value system and its basic message repeatedly and evolved into hate for "the establishment" giving young people the green light to defy authority and do their own thing. Under the protection of poetic license, protesters screamed boldly through their music what would have been over-kill, ludicrous, and terribly offensive in rhetoric alone.

Rock and roll lyrics have encouraged free love and sex outside of marriage, a view of love right out of the Pit. The music has also encouraged free expression which has led to abandonment of inhibitions and resulted in riots and nudity. It is of interest to note that the idea of free expression did not originate with the boomers: 'child development experts' had been advocating this since the mid-1940's.

But contemporary rock is not all "rebellion and immorality." There are many tunes with Christian lyrics. Some say that the use of Christian words with rock tunes resolves the problem in favor of church usage. Such an objection is valid if music is a neutral vehicle. As we have seen in previous chapters, music does not function in a vacuum (where it might be described as amoral), but as a part of culture (where it has moral implications). Foster and a host of others are correct in insisting, "The music has a message."

More to the point is whether rock has moved beyond its original message of defiance and immorality despite the fact there are still immoral lyrics and immoral behavior by secular musicians and devotees. We do well to remember that men sporting beards were once denied access to many Bible Colleges during the 1970's because beards were a sign of rebellion and an immoral lifestyle. Most colleges if not all have repealed that rule.

Can Christian worship and evangelism use the rock musical style that shouts, drives, and rocks back and forth without a clear direction for the future?

The issue may seem moot to some Christian believers, especially boomers and busters since the phrase 'Christian rock' is already an unquestioned part of their vocabulary. Many seniors on the other hand say rock has no place on their agenda ("I will not waste my time even thinking about it") and a newspaper advertisement that touted an evangelical church's use of 'contemporary music' (that is, 'Christian rock' music) as "The Church with Sax Appeal" was a downright turn-off.

ARGUMENTS PRO AND CON

In his book, *The Endless Song, Music and Worship in the Church* (1987), author, professor and musician, Kenneth W. Osbeck quotes Leonard Bernstein's comment on the subject of rock: "Ninety-five percent of this music is likely junk. The other five percent, however, may change the entire future of American music."[3] Osbeck sees beyond rock's superficiality and offers this advice, *"If you really want to understand younger people, you must develop some understanding about their music."*[4]

Osbeck lists arguments for and against the use of rock in church worship. His summary reflects comments commonly heard in discussions about rock:[5]

Proponents justify their position with these arguments:

1. Why should the devil have all of the appealing music?. . . Traditional church music is old-fashioned and irrelevant [to young people]. To attract and keep the younger generation in our churches, we must use music that appeals to them.
2. Just as we must communicate to individuals in language they understand, so we must present the Scriptures and spiritual truths to our young people in forms they understand.
3. Christian rock music gives young people a viable alternative to secular rock. It lets them hear a positive message rather than negative values.
4. Many young people have professed Christ as Savior through the ministry of contemporary music at Christian rock concerts. Christian rock music will give the gospel a hearing with non-Christian young people.
5. Precedents already exist. Christian leaders such as Martin Luther, Charles Wesley, and William Booth of the Salvation Army used the popular music of their day for the texts they wrote.
6. Music is neither sacred nor secular. Therefore, no musical style is inherently evil. The words make the difference. Worthy lyrics sanctify a secular melody.

Opponents respond:

1. Christian rock music is a cheap and distorted representation of biblical Christianity. It is too closely allied with the world's lifestyle. A worthy result never justifies a wrong means.
2. Christian artists who perform this music, though sincere, are using worldly, sensational methods hoping to achieve spiritual results.
3. The words of these songs are usually based on experience. Popular, 'relevant' words may actually be irreverent expressions. Their vague mention of love relationships and commitments could be interpreted as referring to human partners as well as God.
4. The rock music sound is not compatible with the Christian message because it is intrinsically evil. Dr. Howard Hanson, former director of the Eastman School of Music, seeking to disprove the argument

that music itself is amoral or neutral described music with such words as soothing, invigorating, ennobling, vulgarizing, philosophical and orgiastic. He believed it has powers for evil as well as good.

5. Christian rock concerts promote an anti-local church attitude. Christian young people only want to be entertained.
6. Rock style singing is harmful to the voice because it does not use proper vocal techniques.

What is a balanced view?

If we will be objective in evaluating these lists, we must acknowledge there is truth on both sides. Osbeck contends he is not trying to settle the controversy "once and for all." Rather, he offers ten observations, some of which are identical to those reached in this study. In brief, his observations are as follows:[6]

1. The question of finding appropriate musical styles for a local church has never been more divisive.
2. The selection of appropriate musical styles requires discernment by leadership.
3. The music director's ministry is to the whole congregation; personal preference must be laid aside.
4. Musical tastes have a local flavor and those tastes should be recognized and honored.
5. There should be balance in musical styles "that is God-honoring, true to the Scriptures, and aesthetically satisfying to a majority of the congregation."
6. Each song, whether traditional or contemporary, should be judged on its own merits.
7. Periods of spiritual renewal "have always been accompanied with outbursts of Christian song." The 'old-secular' may become the 'new sacred.'
8. To view anything new and unfamiliar or old and traditional as having no merit on those grounds alone is extreme and invalid.
9. There is blessing when a strong, creative spirit is prevalent.
10. We are in danger of losing perspective and must remain clear on the ultimate objectives of a church music ministry.

Different approaches, Different views

There are three major Christian views concerning rock:

1. *Rejection.* Because of association with drugs, loose life styles, rebellion, lyrics, etc., the rock musical style should be rejected without any further discussion.
2. *Acceptance.* Young people are bored with anything but rock, so if the Christian community wishes to reach them, it must open its doors and its arms and welcome 'their music.'
3. *Compromise.* This is the "Spoil-the-Egyptians!" view of Christian psychologist, Dr. Larry Crabb, who suggested this approach for Christian counseling vis-à-vis the many schools of thought in secular psychology.[7] This approach[8] suggests taking "silver, gold and clothing" and leaving "fish, cucumbers, melons, leeks, onions and garlic."[9] However, it may be easier to distinguish gold from garlic than what is good in rock from what is not.

The first approach is wrong. Original rejection was under-standable, but total rejection after the initial furor has blown over is like Christian college orchestra directors who rejected the use of the saxophone prior to the early 1940's because it had been associated with jazz. And it is like Christian colleges who kept the 'no-beard' policy on their books even after beards passed from a mark of rebellion to a fashion statement.

The second approach of *total commitment* to this musical style as the only valid style to express Christian truth is equally unwar-ranted. To assume that a set of Christian words sanctifies any and all musical styles and legitimizes rock as the only valid Christian musical style, is simplistic, intellectually and spiritually indefensible and lacking in discernment. *All Christian truth cannot be poured into one musical style.* For this reason, I have great difficulty accept-ing the label, 'Christian Rock' Concert. We do not expect to pour all the Gospel into the march musical style, nor the waltz, nor the can-tata, nor the symphony, etc. Who ever heard of a Christian concert based on a musical style: "A Christian March Concert"? "A Christian Waltz Concert"?

I believe Dr. Crabb's approach, our third alternative, is correct. Paul told the Corinthian church they had the freedom to eat meat bought in the marketplace: "We know that an idol is nothing at all in the world. . ."[10] However, we do well to remember that there was also a qualifier: "Be careful, however, that the exercise of your freedom does not become a stumbling block to the weak."[11] There are 'qualifiers' when engaging in any Christian behavior and that is true of using the rock musical style as well. We shall examine those qualifiers in the next chapter. Weiss and Tariskin write of Calvin who,

> in his preface to the Geneva Psalter of 1543, quotes from St. Augustine and from Plato on the need to control and regulate music as strictly as possible. For him, as for the medieval Church Fathers, to perform music in church was to play with spiritual fire.[12]

Why the control? Calvin believed there was "a great difference between music that is made to entertain people at home and at table, and the Psalms which are sung in church, in the presence of God and his angels." As noted earlier, Calvin also quoted St. Augustine who wrote that "one must always watch lest a song be light and frivolous; rather, it should have weight and majesty."[13] Since entertainment and sports are perhaps the most prominent features of the contemporary mind-set, how easy it is for immature Christians to expect, even demand, that their religious practices tickle the funny bone and tingle the spine!

ROCK IN THE LIGHT OF CHRISTIAN TRUTH

Rock Music is Loud

We have seen that the rock musical style shouts by its *fortissimo*. Does loud music always imply defiance? The answer is no. It shouts for attention. The *fortissimo* exclaims: "Listener, wake up and pay attention!" Beethoven, Tchaikovsky, Wagner, Bartok and other classical composers knew how to write loud music and most likely none of their music had to do with rebellion.

Composer and conductor, Constant Lambert (1905-1951), an enthusiast in all branches of art but specializing in ballet, comments

on the loud dynamic used in modern classical music. In an enter-
taining collection of pieces, *Music Ho!* published in 1934, he wrote,
"Music has an odd way of reflecting not only the emotional background of an age, but also its physical condition." He noted that the
present age "is one of overproduction," explaining, "Never has there
been so much food and so much starvation, and. . . never has there
been so much music-making and so little musical experience of a
vital order."[14] One would have thought he was describing the last
three decades which he did not live to see! In addressing the issue
of musical dynamics, he wrote:

> We have at present no idea of what havoc may be wrought in
> a few years' time by the combined effect of the noise of city
> life and the noise of city music. . . The noise provided by such
> adjuncts of modern life as the pneumatic drill, the movietone
> news reel and the war film, leaves the most sadistic and
> orgiastic of composers at the starting post. When Berlioz wrote
> the *Symphonie Fantastique* he was providing probably the
> greatest sonority that anyone, including even those military
> men present, had ever heard. When George Antheil adds to
> his score sixteen pianos, an electric buzzer or two, an aero-
> plane propeller, and a pneumatic drill he is, after all, provid-
> ing little more than the average background to a telephone
> conversation. . . We live in an age of tonal debauch where the
> blunting of the finer edge of pleasure leads only to a more
> hysterical and frenetic attempt to recapture it. . . The loud
> speaker is the street walker of music.[15]

What would Lambert have thought of today's sound systems
which pour forth torrents of unrestrained sound? The sound of present "street walkers of music" is more boldly evident than in his day!
Thanks to modern sound systems, most rock music continues loud,
unabated and without relief all the way back to the last row of a
large auditorium. There is no escape because concert-goers are
wrapped in sound that envelopes and batters the eardrums. Some
display a sweet smile of pleasure as sound washes over them like
great waves rolling in on Hawaiian beaches while others bewail
with Lambert the "blunting of the finer edge of sonority."

In defense of contemporary technical developments, it must be
said that the "mechanical music" of the nineteen nineties is so life-
like, it is very nearly like sitting in a concert hall. But the amps are

there to crank up the sound louder than ever before possible! Listeners participate vicariously in the sound and the louder the sound, the greater the 'oneness' (a favorite existential New Age term) *as one succumbs to its effect.*

Why not use loud music in a Christian concert if rebellious words are omitted? The answer to that question is this question: What message is conveyed by loud music apart from rebellious lyrics? Traditional classical composers show that it does not have to be rebellion.

Loud rock music is a shriek or holler akin to yelling, "Pay attention!" If a fire has broken out, one must *yell* "Fire!" not whisper it and no one expects an air raid siren to come in softly and tenderly.

In the counter-culture, rock provides boomers a medium by which they may shout about a society whose values are out of control, resulting in their feelings of being alienated and powerless. And that is perfectly legitimate because it is absolutely true. The musical style is a perfect match.

But two hours yelling, "Fire!"? Hardly! Three hours of a shrieking air raid siren? Lord, spare us!

I do not find it inappropriate for anyone to yell or sound a loud siren when there is reason to do so. More Christians ought to be on the street corners *yelling* warnings (lovingly!) to unbelievers, a practice that has passed into oblivion with the desertion of city downtown areas and the creation of malls which exclude public evangelizing. Christians should be more visible watchmen and get more excited about men and women going to hell! God has a mighty voice and He uses it on occasion!

If the rock musical style can help gain unbelievers' attention like the cry of the word "Fire!" or the word "Snake!" in West Africa, then let's use it! God spoke in the thunder and the earthquake to get His children's attention, so why shouldn't we?

But does that mean the church should have a two-hour concert of *fortissimo?* Of course not. After getting His child's attention by a roll of thunder or a crack of lightening, God often speaks with a still, small voice.[16] Once obtaining our attention, He does not continue to yell, "Attention! Attention! Attention!" by an insistent dinning in our ears. No, He does not continue to attack us with ear-splitting signals or hammer-like blows *because He has our attention.* Then

He speaks of redemption, peace and comfort.

The immoderate use of *fortissimo* in the rock musical style is as unbiblical as the immoderate use of anything else, whether food, drink, or the waltz. Warnings about sin, hell and the coming judgment set to *fortissimo* music is not a mixed message. Putting an ear-splitting rock accompaniment to the message of a gentle and loving Jesus, a meek Lamb going to the cross, or the peace that passes all understanding *is* a mixed message.

Fortissimo music does something else. It eclipses the words. Secular rock artists hide the words from those uninitiated just as an esoteric cult does. For those who could peel back the *fortissimo,* the anti-culture message was there. Sung too distinctly, there would have been objections raised more quickly. The approach was this: capture by the bait—*fortissimo*—then give the new radical message.

If Christian vocalists believe they have a message from the Lord for the congregation, they must exercise control over accompanists and sound people who want to smother lyrics by turning up the volume. Christian vocalists have no hidden, esoteric message to hide; rather, they have every reason to proclaim it with crystal clarity! The Christian message warms the heart, but it does so because it has a rational message that must be heard, received by the mind, and acted upon (cf. Romans 10:14-17).

The Apostle Paul cries out for clarity in worship services and alludes to the bugler, "If the trumpet does not make a clear call, who will get ready for battle?"[17] An audience can only guess at a stage play if the curtains are not drawn. A gift recipient will never know what his or her gift is without unwrapping it. Just so, unbelievers are left to guess what the "greatest story every told" is all about when the *fortissimo* packaging obliterates it.

The argument that rock devotees understand the words even if their elders do not is basically false. Yes, they do understand words to song oldsters cannot, but it is because musical groups send out cassettes and CDs *along with a printed set of the lyrics* before they play a concert in a given location and the young read the words and listen to the music dozens of times.

Loud music is not off-limits to Christians. There is a place for it in the church and for street corners evangelism. Loud music is off-limits only:

(1) if we try to energize the listeners by the power of the sound (and sound can do this) rather than by the power of the Lord;

(2) if there is no contrasting soft music for balance in presenting the *full* Gospel message;

(3) if the loud music is motivated by feelings of defiance and rebellion; and

(4) if the congregation or audience becomes disorderly or is merely entertained and not edified (spiritual discernment is a prerequisite if leadership is to make this distinction).[18]

In the use of the rock musical style, we appeal to the *both/and* concept. The use of *both* loud *and* soft music as the message warrants is appropriate and biblical. An exclusive diet of soft music will put an audience to sleep while an exclusive diet of loud music will dull the senses.

Rock Music has a Driving Beat

This is the second most obvious element that distinguishes rock from other musical styles. The driving beat and the loud dynamic team up together to give a sense of power and produce a feeling that elevates one above his mundane surroundings. It is a great antidote to feelings of powerlessness and boredom though it is temporary and produces inevitable subsequent 'lows.'

Heavily accentuated rhythm is not the sole prerogative of rock music nor does rock have a monopoly on syncopation. There are many classical numbers that use both. 'Upbeat music' is any style of music that moves along at a good tempo and has pronounced rhythm. Neither rhythm nor syncopation is 'of the devil.' How terrible to attribute to the devil what God has given!

Some church groups see strong rhythms, syncopation and bright colors all as contrary to sanctification, implying perhaps unintentionally, "Don't get too happy in the Lord!" Unfortunately, there are still those in the Christian community who feel guilty when they feel happy serving the Lord. Nonsense! God created rhythm, syncopation, bright colors, and joy, too!

Insistent rhythm is not a problem unless it is unrelieved. Even

Beethoven's theme in the first movement of his Fifth Symphony is insistent. I used an insistent rhythm intentionally in a chorus based on Matthew 24:14, "And this gospel of the kingdom shall be preached in all the world for a witness unto all nations; and then shall the end come." The music is *rock-like* in terms of 'beat' but the accompaniment was written to reinforce the message of insistence found in the text.

When Christian artists use pronounced rhythms, they need to do it with extreme caution because stirring up emotions is music's calling. Actually, the church ought to have its emotions more stirred up these days! Christians, however, do not need their emotions stirred up by music to feel better, escape, or be stimulated into a private world of religious ecstasy. To use music in this fashion is to use it as others use mantras, drugs and alcohol.

A musical style using a pronounced rhythmical beat generates power. However, the power for a positive life-changing experience is *never* found in music, but only through that which is "of the Spirit." Power and feelings of well-being generated by such music are temporary, but, more sinister, they are counterfeit substitutes for the real thing. The familiar Gospel song does not insist "'There is power, power, wonder working power' *in a pounding, throbbing sound."*

Addiction to rock and its beat is real. The fundamental meaning of the verb 'to be addicted' is "to be devoted or surrendered to something habitually or obsessively."[19] So long as boomers and busters remain narcissistic and have no other option (so they think erroneously) but to continue to feel powerless and alienated, just so long will they be hooked on rock. Temporary 'power fixes' are addictive and the addiction always cries out for more, and is not healing.

Christians do not need large doses of throbbing music to feel powerful. St. Paul in writing to the Corinthian church said, "We preach Christ crucified. . . Christ the power of God and the wisdom of God."[20] Christ in believers *is* the power of God! Loud throbbing music is not off-limits, but like so many others aspects of life, it must have boundaries.

Rock Music Is Repetitious and Simplistic

We saw that the rock music style uses a short, oft-repeated (*ostinato*) technique, that is, Point A to Point B and back to Point A to Point B. It is doubtful if hard rock ever gets to Point C!

Repetition and a simple music structure is not of the devil any more than loud music or a strong beat. There are examples of both in classical music, secular and sacred. Repetition is easily seen in Beethoven's use of the Morse Code-like dot-dot-dot-dash theme in the first movement of his Fifth Symphony. A well-known example of simplicity in classical music is the nursery rhyme "Twinkle, Twinkle, Little Star" used by Haydn in his Symphony No. 94 ("Surprise").

Redundancy means exceeding what is necessary or normal: for example, using more words than necessary or repeating more often than one would think necessary. Redundancy is not all bad by any means; it is a good teaching technique. Is that a problem? No, not at all. There is redundancy in Christian hymnody, especially in gospel songs, such as "Power in the Blood."

Too much repetition paired with a bare-bones simplistic structure without skillful creativity can backfire. It is boring and suggests 'going nowhere.' It becomes monotonous. I remember a fellow-student's evaluation of a college professor: "She teaches as if we were in kindergarten." Her redundancy technique was overdone and it insulted her students' intelligence.

Is there a social message to rock in this regard? There may be. Many rock songs are repetitious to the point of absurdity. Often, nothing but one short repeated phrase will remain in a listener's mind. If a musical style (a body of art) reflects 'felt life,' then a boring dimension to rock is appropriate because that is one of the boomers' and busters' favorite words, "Boring!" The excitement of the insistent beat and the crashing sound of the loud dynamic make the music exciting, but its basic structure is elementary and repetitious to the point of being—like that college professor—boring. Contradictory though that may sound, both are true. The boring dimension reflects 'felt life,' and the beat allows the listener to rise above it.

The structure and lack of transitional subtleties (moving from one chord to the next) are also extraordinarily simplistic. One major chord may be followed by another major chord without benefit of transition. Dynamic nuances, another factor of complexity, are strikingly missing from the rock musical idiom. The electronic keyboard and audio systems do not lend themselves to subtle shifts from *fortissimo* to *pianissimo*. No, that isn't sinful anymore than are nursery rhymes set to simple tunes—or 'ditties' as we might call the tunes.

Christianity is viewed as simple by babes in Christ, but coming to adulthood in the faith (maturing) shows that Christianity is not simplistic. This is not unlike the contrast between childhood and adulthood in our physical existence.

But true Christianity is not boring; it is an exciting life adventure! Christians do not need something to mirror boredom. The Gospel of Jesus Christ is exciting! It has purpose, goals, direction and great challenges. It is full of spiritual battles, scary valleys and profound mountain-top experiences. For those who think it is boring and an old monotonous tale, let them show me their Gospel by their two-hour rock concert of ONE-ONE-ONE-ONE or THUMP-THUMP-THUMP-THUMP and I will show them my Gospel by my slow music *paired with* my up-tempo music, by my gentle rhythm *and* my insistent rhythm, by my appeal to the mind *and* my appeal to the heart!

Yes, we can use redundancy and repetition for they have merit as teaching tools, but we cannot use repetition as a 'Christian mantra' to manipulate feelings for the purpose of creating an emotional high no matter how delightful that momentary high may be. If rock or "Just as I Am without One Plea"[21] (remember those long altar calls?) or any other style of music is used in this fashion, it degrades the Gospel and trivializes His Kingdom.

An effective speaker who wants to drive a point home tells what he is going to talk about, tells it, and concludes by reviewing what he talked about. He has built in a lot of redundancy, but when done skillfully, the method is effective. Redundancy and repetition are not anti-Christian in speech or in music and there is surely time and place for a moderate use of the rock's repetitious musical style.

Rock Music: Emotional Content

Rock is faulted because it has a high emotional content and can produce something akin to ecstasy. So can many classical selections. And so can some invitation hymns. I have emphasized more than once that God created emotions and that emotions and worship are not enemies. God never intended either feelings or excitement to be banished from public worship and the psalms testify to that.

Rock has a strong emotional punch and the problem with it is not that one number has a high emotional content, but that one rock number with high emotional content follows another with the same high emotional content which in turn follows another, and yet another. An hour or two of music with high emotional content, rock or otherwise, is not merely excessive, but downright dangerous. The problem for Christians is not emotion or a highly-emotional musical style, but the immoderate use of it.

Unfortunately, some Christians only get excited when seated on hard stadium seats in the hot sun for two to three hours while watching a small pigskin ball thrown back and forth between two groups of grown men whose faces are hid by protective helmets. A young college friend was so excited that his softball team made it to the finals, he had no objection to playing several games in a single day about twenty five miles from home: game number one at 9:30 a.m., game number two at 1:30 p.m., game number three (after a round of golf) at 7 p.m. and game number four at 11:45 p.m. He did not finish that game as he tore some ligaments in his knee at 12:30 a.m. Hobbling on crutches the next day, was he ready to give up softball? I should say not! He was all smiles because as he tore up his knee, he was safe at home. We do not let affliction deter us from our heart's desire!

Some people get excited about sports, some get "high" on rock, but how many Christians become enthusiastic about the Lord? How many are willing to take half the night to witness to a believer, and though, feeling 'dead' the next day, rejoice despite the weariness because a sinner came 'home'? Where is our heart? That should be a question of great concern to every Christian and especially to church leadership.

It is clear from Psalm 46 that there is a time to cease striving and be quiet before the Lord. Psalm 47 tells us there is also a time to show one's emotions outwardly and publicly: "clap. . . shout." No one was happier in public than King David as he danced before the ark when he had it brought back to Jerusalem. Perhaps we can say that those who would dampen public expressions of feelings in worship are afflicted with the Michal syndrome[22] which was fatal to her.

At times singing and sharing must reflect celebration, and at other times a quiet solemnity. The celebration concept, so common in most of the Jewish holydays celebrated at the Temple in Jerusalem, is a thought foreign to many who plan Christian worship services. There are two trends today. The first is to crank up the hoopla and celebrate, and the second is to make all worship quiet and meditative (no noise in the sanctuary!). Both extremes are wrong.

Too much display of emotions and too little solid teaching of the Word that challenges the mind is too much fluff, too little substance, and trouble ahead for the local church. On the other hand, too little emotion is to convert the sanctuary into a funeral parlor.

The answer to church renewal is not found in a philosophy that says, "Youth are the future of the church, therefore, we must do whatever it takes to make it their church." The church is the church of seniors, boomers *and* busters and a renewal plan must balance the needs of all three sub-cultures. The wisdom of the aged must not be squelched in favor of the enthusiasm of the young, nor must the freshness and creativity of the young be rejected in favor of the experience of the aged.

True Christianity is not Dullsville but rather an exciting adventure that includes travel (the Great Commission), spiritual muscle-building (growing in the grace and knowledge of our Lord) and 'military' involvement (spiritual warfare). Christians have a great Leader and a power that cannot fail. One dear friend whom I knew for a number of years would shake his head once in a while as I recounted something the Lord was doing, and say, "You certainly live an exciting life." Not always, of course, but the down times are far offset by the up times. This is what boomers and busters need to hear verbally and musically when they come to church.

When music serves as a vehicle for truth that edifies the heart, it functions legitimately and with integrity. The rock musical style can function in such a way and help the Christian express his or her feelings of praise, celebration and joy. Rock as a musical style, however, is like whipped cream which must be used sparingly. When it is used to create an emotional encounter or, as they say, when it is pure hype, it is sensationalism and worse, commercialism. This is not Christian.

1. A constant diet of the truth of God sung only to a musical style with the *loud dynamic* as found in rock, will confirm the notion that the words of the Gospel, the rational content, is secondary to a person's personal existential experience of the Gospel.
2. A constant diet of the truth of God sung only to a musical style that has a *strong insistent beat* as is found in rock, will confirm the notion that the source of power is in the music rather than from the Holy Spirit, and that its hypnotic beat, causing reality to fade, is the source of 'cleansing.'
3. A constant diet of the truth of God sung only to a musical style with a *simple structure and much repetition* such as is found in rock, will confirm the notion that the Gospel is neither deep nor complex and the goal is less important than a subjective experience.
4. A constant diet of the truth of God sung only to a musical style with a *strong emotional content* such as is found in rock, can induce loss of control and a movement into psychological rather than spiritual ecstasy.

Martin Luther notes music's persuasive power in rather descriptive, almost amusing terms, and gives warning concerning those who would abuse this gift from the Lord:

> Those who are the least bit moved know nothing more amazing in the world. But any who remain unaffected are clodhoppers indeed and are fit to hear only the words of dung-poets and the music of pigs. . . Take special care to shun perverted minds who prostitute this lovely gift of nature and of art with their erotic rantings; and be quite assured that none but the devil goads them on to defy their very nature which would and should praise God its maker with this gift, so that these bastards purloin the gift of God and use it to worship the foe of God, the enemy of nature and of this lovely art.[23]

Paul balances the truth of the individual's marvelous freedom in Christ with the law of love: Permissible? Yes, but not everything is beneficial, constructive or edifying. The following topics say something about important qualifiers in the use of rock by Christians: Expectations, Fit, Association and Borrowing.

Expectations

At the conclusion of a funeral service, the funeral director made his customary remarks following my final "Amen." As the guests began to file past the casket for the last time, the "Chattanooga Choo-Choo" began making its way across our consciousness. I was a bit startled and mystified as to its source. The shrill 'choo-choo' was coming from the ceiling speakers.

We have a certain set of expectations concerning the use of music at particular events in our lives. Traditionally, many cultures—ours included—dictate slower music for funerals and faster for celebrations. We make such associations not merely because of tradition but because of the way we think about death and celebration. Our expectations lead us to the assumption that certain musical styles go with particular events but not necessarily with others.[24]

It is likely most Americans believe the "Chattanooga Choo-Choo" is not quite appropriate for a funeral, a graduation or a wedding processional, but not out of place at a fun-gathering or a dance where oldsters in particular want to enjoy remembering the big band sounds of Glenn Miller.

Later I was told the number was in honor of the elderly bereaved spouse who loved Glenn Miller's orchestra. He was "not much of a church-goer," family members said, so the boomers in the family decided this would please him. And it did.

Someone has said, "Anything goes today." True, but those over forty years of age still don't expect to see a velvet jacket and black tie worn with jeans nor a woman attending the New York Metropolitan Opera House dressed exceptionally well, including a fur coat, but with curlers in her hair.[25] The defense is, "C'mon, get with it! The times they are a-changin'!"

Who is to say that a song which honored and pleased an old

man was inappropriate? The boomers broke with tradition (and that is the beauty of boomers—they are not enslaved to it), but they did it in a context of love at least for the elderly gentleman, if not for the rest of us. The pastor and guests would have been less startled if the family had made an announcement before the train left the station!

Since the major concern of every believer is love and not tradition, expectations do not need to be defended at all cost. Jesus' words to the Pharisees in a number of Gospel passages is a commentary on this. When such behavior is explained to us in this fashion, that is, relating it to a context of love rather than self satisfaction, the affront to our expectations can be, should be, dispelled.

But iconoclasts tearing down all tradition cannot be defended either. Such behavior devastates. Tradition takes shape naturally so the behavior in a culture is neither totally random nor confronted with new information at every turn—a totally intolerable situation. Tradition shapes expectations and habits. Our rising in the morning, bathing, brushing our teeth, and so on, are really part of personal tradition. There are certain things we expect to do, and habit, a child of tradition, helps us do them efficiently and requires less brain and emotional energy.

We do not expect to see mourners attired in bathing suits at a funeral. Tradition helps us retain our sanity by organizing the world around us more efficiently and providing a degree of security. The new is akin to the unknown and that is more scary.

Change will come whether or not we like it, but it can come more easily for older people when they are convinced a suggested change is in deference to a high cause—love. They are able then to tolerate the new.

Traditions, expectations, and habits may be wrong, or simply no longer efficient for present times. Then they become the diseased appendix our body no longer needs. Church renewal must excise the poison. Some expectations need to go if church renewal is to be successful, but leadership must be as careful as a surgeon with a scalpel.

To alter the analogy, changes in church musical style (and hopefully changes to a more balanced presentation) cannot act as a barbaric army does entering a town, indiscriminately shooting everyone and everything on sight. A lot of damage is done with this kind of approach. It is irreparable, inexcusable, and unbiblical.

Successful change in the church is more than removal of failed expectations and implementation by leadership of fresh, new ideas. It is a process of instructing congregations so their expectations, often found at the subconscious level, may be identified and reshaped to meet current needs.

FIT

Since lyrics say something and music also communicates a message of its own, we can assume a good fit results when musical style complements lyrics. A poor fit conveys two separate, often contradictory messages.

Luther was aware that music of his day apart from lyrics had a message of its own and he struggled with fit between lyrics and musical style. When he was arranging the German mass at Wittenburg, he requested the help of two musicians, Conrad Rupff and Michael Prætorius, so a decision could be made concerning which 'mode' (or loosely, style) to use. After visiting Luther, Prætorius (1571-1621) later wrote about the visit in his three-volume musical encyclopedia, *Syntagma musicum:*

> We talked to him [Luther] at length about church music and the nature of the eight modes. At length he assigned the eighth mode to the Epistle, and the sixth to the Gospel, saying, "Christ is a most amiable Lord, his words are sweet; let us, therefore, use the sixth mode for the Gospel. St. Paul, on the other hand, is a grave and serious apostle; let us use the eighth mode for the Epistle."[26]

Luther was concerned there be a correct fit to avoid dissonance between music and lyrics. A poem on thunder set to a musical accompaniment of gentle flute sounds and a pastoral scene pictured by dissonant, unresolved, crashing chords send garbled messages. The signals of musical accompaniment must be consistent with the signals verbalized in song just as Christians are to be sure their behavior sends the same signal they convey in their verbal testimony. There is great danger in reflecting a non-Christian world view of dissonance which occurs when immature Christian musicians pattern their composition and performance after the techniques of the world.

Schaeffer has warned us that this is an age of distortion and fragmentation. He illustrates the contention clearly in his description of the flow of the arts as we saw in a previous chapter. He points out that this trend is apparent in painting, sculpture, architecture, film and music. Those who have lost God have also lost coherence and unity. Many strive through Eastern mysticism to become one with the universe, but without God that is always doomed to failure. There is nothing left but meaninglessness and dissonance.

One important reminder: a new hymnody is distinctly Christian when it has a style that reflects Christian thought and life experiences. A line needs to be drawn somewhere, a line very similar to that line contemporary American church leaders must draw between orthodoxy and heresy so as to avoid theological syncretism.

ASSOCIATION AND BORROWING

When the very catchy song, "Roll Out the Barrel (And We'll Have a Barrel of Fun)" became popular during the early 1940's, a Christian evangelist put a set of Christian words to the melody and sang it at a Christian college. It provoked confusion because when the music started, the original words automatically started to play back in the students' minds. It was a fun tune paired with an objectionable message to evangelicals. Now it was being paired to a very serious message concerning Jesus Christ. Was the soloist to be taken seriously? More importantly, was the message he was singing to be taken seriously?

Don't Christian words 'sanctify' a tune? They may, but not always. Christian words did not sanctify that melody at that time and in that setting because of the matter of *association.* The original song was too recent and it was at a time when most evangelical churches had a code of behavior that proscribed both drinking and dancing.

Also, the musical style was such that only a very special set of words appropriate to the style could be used effectively—if and when the original words were forgotten. The result was dissonant and jarring. The flow of worship was interrupted by an unexpected intruder.

Folk tunes have a sort of historical reality to them and generally only bring smiles when paired with Christian words. The original lyrics do not stimulate strong feelings. *Londonderry Air* has several sets of Christian words, and many of Stephen Foster's songs are paired with Christian lyrics, for example, the chorus of "Old Black Joe." The original message was nearly neutral in terms of emotional impact.

Does the practice of borrowing contemporary tunes for the Christian hymnody have good solid precedent? "Luther did it!" "Wesley did it!" Their alleged practice is used by some today to justify using the rock musical style.

In researching the issue, I failed to find any support for the claim that Luther used popular barroom tunes of the day to present the Gospel. There is no support that Wesley did either. Luther is 'quoted' by Weiss and Taruskin (and others) as saying he could not see why the devil should have all the best tunes.[27]

The record indicates Luther had a very high regard for music; he himself was a fine musician. If anything, he went the high road and sought what he thought was the best in music in order to glorify the Lord. Luther encouraged German poets "to compose evangelical hymns for us" but he also complained about some of the new music: "Few [new songs] are found that are written in a proper devotional style."[28] It is doubtful he would have sanctioned "Roll Out the Barrel" or "Chattanooga Choo-Choo" for use in worship.

Wesley took only two or three folk tunes of the day to use as accompaniments for Christian lyrics. We need also to be aware that folk tunes of that day were something different from that which the term 'barroom tunes' implies (bawdy, often obscene, etc.). In small towns in England the 'pub' (public house) was—and still is—a place for the exchange of information and exercising neighborliness. What is a barroom in America? It is an establishment "whose main feature is a bar for the sale of liquor."[29]

It was the Salvation Army that used the popular tunes of the day. This practice, which started back in the latter half of the nineteenth century continues today. Moyles says the founder, General William Booth, set the tone. It was Booth, not Luther or Wesley, who said:

Secular music, do you say? Belongs to the devil, does it? Well, if it did, I would plunder him of it, for he has no right to a single note of the whole gamut. . . Every note and every strain and every harmony is divine, and belongs to us.[30]

Booth's philosophy encouraged Salvationists to use any and every popular melody. Early in the history of the Salvation Army, a set of Christian words was set by a Salvationist to the "popular music-hall tune," called "Champagne Charlie," and this started the trend "which would characterize Salvation Army songs for many years to come." Other popular borrowed tunes were, "The Girl I Left Behind Me," "Oh Dear, What Can the Matter Be?" "Just Before the Battle, Mother," "Close the Shutters, Willie's Dead" and "The Wearin' of the Green." Their repertoire also included melodies such as, "Beautiful Dreamer," "Flow Gently, Sweet Afton," "Swanee River," "Home on the Range," and "Old Folks at Home."

Moyles says that by November 1884, "this sort of purloining had become an accepted practice, and almost every Canadian Salvationist seemed to be trying his or her hand at song-writing." The practice of putting "'heavenly' words to secular tunes became very popular." It was quite a break with tradition, a novelty in its day. One of the founders of the Canadian corps, Jack Addie, composed over one hundred such songs, including a parody of this practice, entitled, "The Songs I used to Sing":

> To think about the pardoned past,
>   Oft to my mind does bring
> The happy times I thought I had,
>   The songs I used to sing.
> Once I was blind but now I see,
>   I want the world to know
> That I've learned to sing far better songs
>   Than those of long ago.
>
> There was "Captain Jinks of the Horse Marines,"
>   And "Comin' Thro' the Rye,"
> "A Ramble on a Starry Night,"
>   "Wait 'Till the Clouds Roll By."
> "We Won't Go Home 'Till Morning," and
>   "The Reg'lar Army, Oh!"
> But I've learned to sing far better songs
>   Than those of long ago.

Moyles adds, "It was, in fact, the 'jolly singing' of Salvationists which attracted many outsiders to the Army meetings." By 1882, the year a corps was founded in Canada, the Salvation Army "had evolved its own peculiar brand of music with songs to match" and Salvationists, we are told, recognized each other by the music they sang. In those days, "Salvationists never sang hymns," according to Moyles, but used traditional and secular melodies *to attract unbelievers to their street corner meetings.* Moyles says with relief, "Many of these songs (happily the worst) enjoyed but a brief moment of popularity."[31]

I found an interesting example of rock borrowing from classical music when my opinion on rock was sought out by a senior high Sunday School class. After hearing the selection, I also found the answer to a question I had often wondered about—and others have asked me about: do young people really hear the lyrics while we older folks don't because we're not tuned in, and simply, we're not 'with it'?

The rock selection played for me was based on *Etude in C Minor* by Chopin, and was clearly a mating of the classical and rock styles. David Meece is credited with the arrangement and he performed the number skillfully.[32] Chopin may well have turned over in his grave (as they say), but the selection was pure virtuosity. This was no traditional, simplistic, three-chord rock number. It was rock-like because of the steady, insistent rhythm and the unrelieved loud dynamic that prevailed during the singing. The skillful performance, the tempo and the beat left one breathless. It had variations in tempo with three contrasting themes that unfortunately, in my opinion, seemed disconnected. But as we learned earlier, fragmentation and discontinuity are also a hallmark of this present age and the rock and contemporary classical musical styles. On closer examination, I found the simplistic Christian lyrics not at all well-suited to the musical style.

As it turned out, not one of the young people in the class had heard this music before. *Nor could any student tell me a single word of the lyrics after hearing it for the first time!* When I questioned them about how they knew the words to other songs, they answered that groups generally promoted their audio cassettes first—and lyrics are included with the cassette.

How then, I wondered, could a concert—billed as a Christian Rock Concert with evangelism as its goal—ever challenge the heart and mind of the unsaved when they do not understand the message of the lyrics? The answer is, of course, if they cannot understand the lyrics, the music is nothing more than pure entertainment. The words, Christian though they may be, cannot impact listeners who have not been previously exposed to the lyrics. Only the break in the concert for Christian testimonies by the musicians can provide any evangelistic thrust. The question is whether hearts are truly ready for the call of the Master in a context of entertainment.

So what do we do about rock and rock-like musical styles? Can evangelicals approve and use them or not? *Yes, we can, but very carefully. Like a baker using spices.*

Setting Boundaries

*Let the wise listen and add to their
learning and let the discerning get guid-
ance.*

Solomon

D on't use a knife when you need a screwdriver! Never use
your teeth when you need a pair of pliers! Using the right
tool makes one more efficient and less apt to fall victim to
a bit of unhappiness at best or real tragedy at the worst. The carpenter in building a piece of furniture requires more than one tool,
and so does the musician in building up the Body of Christ. Just as
the carpenter needs training in the use of his tools, so too do musicians.

A musician's tools include the skillful use of his or her voice,
finger dexterity on an instrument, the ability to read music, a knowledge of musical styles, etc. Musical styles are tools that can be used
properly or improperly, too.

How can we use the rock musical style to glorify God? To
answer that question, I will summarize the differences in the
Christian and secular world views for which musical styles are the
objectification of 'felt life,' suggest guidelines for general church
renewal and for church music, and conclude with specific advice for
parents.

SUMMARY STATEMENT OF WORLD VIEWS

Christian World-View

The Christians' music is an objectification of Christian ideas and
concepts. Therefore Christian music will be—and must be—different.
If it is not, a charge of syncretism would be in order.

What are some of the key Christian words or concepts? For
starters, the list of the fruit of the Spirit will answer that question nicely: "Love, Joy, Peace, Patience, Kindness, Goodness, Faithfulness,

Gentleness, and Self-control."[1] To this we may add: sin, hell, heaven, devil, condemnation, damnation, watchman, shepherd, etc.

Counter-Culture World View

Key words or concepts turn up again and again in the boomers' and busters' vocabulary and we should therefore not be surprised to find them incorporated into the counter-culture's art forms. The lyrics are replete with them and its music is manipulated to reflect and support them.

Some of these words or concepts are: fear, rebellion, demand for attention, violence, indulgence, escape, bluntness ('honesty'), lack of courtesy, I, me, distress, desperation, despair, depression, meaninglessness, alienation, loneliness, isolation, and so on. If this is the way members of the counter-culture feel, then the objectification of those feelings generated by this world view will be—and is—evident in their art.

However, we must not write off the counter-culture because it handled its demands for change badly. Here is a summary of some of the positive ideas and values this movement brought to light:

1. The counter-culture identified the bankruptcy (and hypocrisy) of the prevalent assumption that science along with its pals, education and economy, could usher in the golden age of peace and prosperity. The counter-culture rejected the importance of college and material gain and promoted a more simple, casual lifestyle. The effect was felt by colleges, some of which thought seriously about offering bicycles to entice high school graduates to enter college.

2. The counter-culture forced the society to accept the fact that public expression of feelings is not improper and unwholesome.

3. The counter-culture proclaimed the virtue of a number of positive but neglected values (noted earlier) such as equality, spontaneity, the individual, etc. But alas, the 'new order' became as unbalanced as the 'old order'!

4. The counter-culture forced science to come to terms with the supernatural as a valid field of inquiry, and in so doing,

raised serious doubts about the validity of the philosophy of scientism. (Science now accepts para-psychology as a legitimate field for research, and has shown an interest in after-death experiences, miracles, and other assorted supernatural phenomena. Unfortunately, the New Age movement is rushing in to fill the vacuum created by the rejection of science as the only source of knowledge.)

GENERAL PRINCIPLES

The following general principles are foundational if we are to set boundaries for church music. These principles are biblically defensible and workable and, when made part of a philosophy of change for church renewal, will prove profitable to those churches that desire to avoid both syncretism and conflict. The rationale for these principles is found in previous chapters.

PRINCIPLE 1 - CHANGE IS A FACT OF LIFE

Church music has experienced one change after another. The New Testament church music was not just like the Old Testament Temple music, nor was the music in either the early church period or the later period the same as that which preceded it. Expressions of art reflect or mirror cultural changes, and there have been a number of extreme cultural changes and art styles over the centuries!

Contemporary faithful church leaders must work diligently in our present age if they are to maintain stability and security in the midst of rapid, even mind-boggling cultural changes. A congregation often finds it easier to talk about change than actually change. A program of patient teaching that change is not harmful and destructive but rather healthy and life-sustaining when based on the Word of God is of primary importance. The church through the ages could not escape change but the church did not suffer when change was handled wisely.

Faithful church leaders teach a changeless Christ, but they must also teach that *growth is change*. Growth always means new responsibilities, new challenges, and adaptation. When congregants mature because of good teaching, they will change. A happy small church with strong leadership will grow numerically, and, making changes to accommodate that growth, will sustain that growth. Many small churches grow only to lose that growth and chiefly because they are unwilling to make the necessary changes for accommodation.

Growth spiritually, numerically, and financially all challenge the status quo. If a church is a growing church, change is at the door, ready or not! It will be met with concern but must be welcomed as a friend. Teaching biblical principles with much patience so as to make clear what is needed and why, dispels the fear of the unknown for those whose security is as much in the status quo as it is in the Lord. Just as we cannot prevent Junior's growing spurt—even though it means new clothes and new shoes—so we cannot prevent change from affecting the church. Nor should any thinking Christian want to.

PRINCIPLE 2 - ALL CHANGE MUST BE DONE FOR GOD'S GLORY

There is nothing more foundational for any Christian philosophy than St. Paul's ringing exhortation to the first-generation Corinthian church: "So whether you eat or drink or whatever you do, do it all for the glory of God."[2] Later Paul reminds them that "all reflect the Lord's glory [and] are being transformed into his likeness with ever-increasing glory, which comes from the Lord, who is the Spirit."[3]

What is our basic motivation in renewal? Do whatever it takes to fill up the seats and the offering plates? Do whatever it takes to bring in the unsaved? Do whatever it takes to bring in the young? Do whatever it takes to make sinners feel better about themselves as a sort of pre-evangelism softening-up technique? God's truth has not changed: the end still does not justify the means. Our senior generation was entirely wrong in calling the first part of a worship service *preliminaries,* but they were absolutely right in highlighting the centrality of the Word. Unfortunately while pulpits got larger, depth of teaching tended to get more shallow! Today, the emphasis is on the first part of the service, especially music, and the remainder of the service, the preaching, is an add-on.

To find out how 'successful' a church is, we hear questions like this, "How many attended last Sunday morning?" Or, "How big is your Sunday School?" Or, "How much does your church give to missions?" Numbers are helpful, but putting numbers ahead of 'God's glory' is carnal. The numbers game is dangerous because it is so subtle. Jesus' primary motive in all He did was to please the Father. He said so plainly, "I always do what pleases Him,"[4] and it had little to do with numbers. He attracted a crowd, but He also let both the crowd and the rich young ruler depart (with sadness, the Gospel writer notes). At the crucifixion, no one stood to His defense, but He was pleasing the Father. Today, standing totally alone is not equated with success.

PRINCIPLE 3 - ALL CHANGE MUST BE SPIRITUAL

This flows naturally from the previous principle and almost seems redundant. But it must be added. Leadership must ensure that each member of the congregation is developing in the basic spiritual disciplines so that each one will be equipped to do "the work of ministry" as Paul instructed the Ephesian elders. Remember Hebrews 6:1-3 which begins, "Therefore let us leave the elementary teachings about Christ and go on to maturity. . ."

Maturing believers increase in their love for one another and, for them, change becomes far less disruptive.

PRINCIPLE 4 - ALL CHANGE MUST BE CHARACTERIZED BY BALANCE

No policy statement of change can be thoroughly spiritual unless there is balance. For example, all our speech must be to the glory of God, which results in a commitment to speak the truth always. But speaking the truth is not spiritual if it is not balanced with love. The Apostle's exhortation bears repeating: "Speak the truth *in love."* (Ephesians 4:12).

Love means that church policies affecting seniors must be balanced with policies affecting boomers and busters. A proposed change for one group must not be to the hurt of another group within the church. A spiritually based philosophy has equal concern for *both* females *and* males, *both* the major ethnic group *and* any minority groups within a church, *both* singles *and* marrieds, *both* young *and* old, and *both* poor *and* rich.

If a local church does not actively promote love and tolerance, each group will vie for recognition, demand a larger share of the budget, and set up a wail if this is not forthcoming. The result of such carnal behavior is confrontation and polarization. Remember, it is not spiritual to insist that seniors within the church swallow their preferences and forget their needs, or to insist the younger generation be seen but not heard. Policies which encourage division are deficient in the most crucial spiritual value of all—love. Love obviates what some churches see as a necessity: traditional services for the older, contemporary services for the younger.

Spiritual balance means understanding issues that are either/or versus those that are both/and. Christians who have a better grasp of balance as expressed in the both/and concept will find themselves more tolerant and more joyful. The either/or approach to planning often polarzies between: "Everything is planned here; there are no surprises!" and "We plan nothing; we let the Spirit lead!" This divides a church into opposing camps quicker than differences in theology.

An eclectic both/and view to worship requires a degree of tolerance—often a missing virtue. One church indicated it tried the eclectic approach—that is, selecting what was best in various methods or styles—and later abandoned it as unworkable. They then based their worship musical style on the kind of music the majority of the somewhat youthful congregation preferred. That was determined by finding out what radio station they listened to. (I need not report that many younger people don't generally listen to Christian radio stations.) They reported that this was working out well.

However, the eclectic approach can work. It will not work where love for others who are not quite like me nor have tastes quite like mine is in short supply. The key to a mature spiritual balance is love.

PRINCIPLE 5 - PERCEIVED NEEDS ARE NOT THE BASIS FOR CHANGE

The unsaved and the spiritually immature will express perceived needs which they feel deeply, and a local church must not arbitrarily dismiss them. However, perceived needs are not the deciding factor in making changes.

For example, a child may express very strongly what he or she perceives to be a critical need. Sometimes it is difficult to keep from smiling when a child has found manipulative vocabulary and pleads with pathos and tears, "But I *need* it!" Now take a look at his 'perceived need,' and I present two scenarios: (1) the 'it' is Super-Nintendo and he believes he desperately needs it because all his friends have one; or (2) the 'it' is a pair of new shoes because the soles of the shoes are full of holes. What will the child opt for?

The pressing need of every unbeliever (and many believers too) is generally not what they perceive. It may not be prayer (as I once instructed a professing Christian whose voice was full of pathos as he tearfully pled for prayer support), but obedience. The Bible defines a sinner's basic need as redemption which God has provided in Jesus Christ.

The responsibility of the church is to uncover the rottenness of the heart, not to cover it up or excuse it. The duty of the church is to call for repentance of sinners and 'faith-stretching' of saints. And what an uncomfortable feeling those exhortations generate! A doctor does no patient a service by offering more pleasant surroundings and a cushioned seat while hiding a diagnosis of an inner cancer. I doubt the patient will handle the knowledge that he has cancer more tolerably simply because he has a more comfortable chair or is seated in an air conditioned office.

Some churches vote to have a service of all rock or rock-like music on the basis of need. Here are two lines of thought: (1) we need the young, and they like the music, so let's go for it; or (2) young people need rock so we must meet their need. The perceived need of the crowd on Palm Sunday was to free themselves from the yoke of Rome. Jesus did not cater to that need.

On the day of Pentecost, Peter did not make the crowd 'feel good' as he preached to them. He said directly, "This man [Jesus] was handed over to you by God's set purpose and foreknowledge; and you, with the help of wicked men, put him to death by nailing him to the cross." What effect did that have on the crowd? "When the people heard this, they were cut to the heart." Did that make the cause of evangelism suffer? No! They cried out, "Brothers, what shall we do?" The text tells us that Peter "warned them; and he pleaded with them." The result? "About three thousand" were converted in one day![5] This was not a time for telling jokes or falling off a chair under the influence of what has come to be called 'holy laughter.' Although this should not be interpreted to mean that up-tempo music is un-Christian, it is to say that it would have been inappropriate here. This was a solemn moment.

PRINCIPLE 6 - KNOWLEDGE OF PERCEIVED NEEDS IS ESSENTIAL

Does this sound like double-talk since Principles 5 and 6 seem to contradict each other? Not at all. Principle 5 tells us that perceived needs of unbelievers (or believers for that matter) are not the *basis* for a presentation of Gospel truth. Principle 6 encourages discovery of suitable points of contact. A fine line perhaps, but a critical one.

St. Paul knew something about the Athenians when he stood up to preach his sermon (Acts 17) because he took time to walk through the city and see its devotion to Greek gods. There were idols and altars at many of the intersections in the city, including one dedicated to "The Unknown God." Paul used that information as a point of contact in the presentation of the Gospel message. He began with their perceived need, using it as a starting point, and then skillfully bridged the chasm between their secular world view and perceived needs to that of the Christian world view. He helped them relate to a truth he knew would be difficult for them, the resurrection of Christ, by quoting a well-known secular poet who called mankind the 'offspring' of God.

Paul did not hand out lollipops, coupons for free admission to the next lecture, nor provide them with cushions as they sat in the hot sun on Mars Hill's hard rocks. He did not entertain them or try to make them feel better other than letting them know he understood some of their longings. Rather, he confronted them with the uncomfortable 'hard truth' of the resurrection, uncomfortable because it challenged their world view to its core. He presented them with a challenge that demanded a verdict.

Paul traveled by land and sea to come to them. He took time to notice their fallen and sad condition. He went to them and met them on their ground—literally—where they were more comfortable. But, after building a bridge to them, he invited them to cross it.

This doesn't exhaust the list of principles, but it provides a good start for those interested in pursuing a Christian philosophy for church renewal.

GUIDELINES FOR CHURCH MUSIC

We may now turn our attention to principles for change relating to church music. As we move on to these principles, we do well to remember that Plato, Aristotle, Augustine, Luther, Calvin all believed there was a *music-world view connection* and there was therefore danger in accepting musical styles willy-nilly. We still hear occasional warnings from our contemporaries.

For example, in *Ministry and Musicians,* William Hooper says, "Music has the ability to move people both emotionally and intellectually," and, "herein lies both the strength and weakness of church music," for "the music produced in church could become an end in itself rather than a means to an end." This he says is true when "emotional and intellectual stimulation is all that is produced or required." He concludes, "Such a situation could result in the loss of real spiritual power that could come through music."[6]

PRINCIPLE 1 - THE ARTS REFLECT OR MIRROR THE WAY LIFE FEELS AND A BODY OF CHRISTIAN ART IS THE OBJECTIFICATION OF CHRISTIAN (SPIRITUAL) FEELINGS

Our first principle is the basic premise discovered in earlier chapters. True Christian music, not just the lyrics but the musical style as well, is an objectification of a Christian world view and accompanying feelings which has at its center redemption and hope in Christ. Any body of music that purports to be Christian but conveys a message of distortion and dissonance and lacks a solid Christology in the lyrics, misses the mark (a definition, by the way, of sin). And there is a lot of this kind of music around today!

The seriousness of the problem is two-fold: the musician conveying such a so-called Christian message is out of touch with Christ, and worse, any audience welcoming such music is out of touch with Christ as well—and is being led further astray since art also functions to reinforce a world view.

A musician who is truly spiritual also functions as a Christian prophet, and as such, rejects the carnal feelings of his audience and presents an alternate message, persisting in it if his audience is less than enthusiastic—and even if he is unable to make it big in the recording world. Like prophets of old, many skilled artists lived in the not-so-proverbial attics ('garrets') and nearly starved, achieving recognition after they were dead! And who wants that kind of life? Isaiah, Jeremiah, and Ezekiel all wrestled with it, but persisted so as to please God.

PRINCIPLE 2 - *CHRISTIAN MUSIC AND SECULAR MUSIC MUST DIFFER FROM EACH OTHER BECAUSE EACH REFLECTS A DIFFERENT SET OF FEELINGS AND WORLD VIEW*

The Christian and secular world views are poles apart and their respective musical styles will differ from each other because music reflects the way each feels about life. Italian music reflects the way Italians view life, and German music mirrors the German world view. Just so, mature Christians like mature Christian music and carnal Christians like carnal music. What is 'carnal' music? It is music which makes one feel good but focuses the listener on him- or herself rather than on God and Christ. It does not build one up in the most holy faith because it lacks the edification quality and instead projects an entertainment quality.

PRINCIPLE 3 - *MUSIC THAT IS DIFFERENT IS NOT NECESSARILY CHRISTIAN BECAUSE IT IS DIFFERENT*

Christian composers are not locked into a musical style simply because the style is different from that of the world or because some Christian communities label the style as 'Christian music.' Nor does all Christian music have to sound the same, a fear entertained by some. Christians composers are not required to write in the style of the Gregorian chant or hymns or praise choruses. These forms are different from secular music but that is not what makes them Christian.

Composers tuned in to God find He is superlatively creative. Just view the numberless varieties of life around us, the result of His creative abilities! Surely creativity is not the prerogative of the sinner. In fact, the sinner's creativity is limited because his or her world view is! God's creative hand has been evident in the John Peterson-style cantatas and, more recently, in the 'praise chorus' style that has proven to be a great assist to private and public worship. There is much that is inferior, but there is also much that is very good.

The problem is not new creative forms, but the snobbishness that accompanies something old and traditional and contrariwise, snobbishness that accompanies something new when either is held up as the only acceptable form of worship.

PRINCIPLE 4 - OLD MUSICAL FORMS NEVER PRECLUDE THE CREATION OF NEW FORMS

We examined the history of Church music and saw that changes have occurred in church music over the ages. New spiritual insights and the pressures of a changing culture contributed to these changes. To view new music with caution is to act appropriately, but to reject the new simply because it is new is evidence of immaturity. As always, spiritual discernment is of paramount importance.

Let's remember Neill Foster's warning, "Discernment seems to have failed utterly when confronted with stiffened prejudice and the resolute will." He adds,

> Such failure is reason enough then to seek before God to be as pliable and unprejudiced before Him as it is possible to be, and reason enough also to say that the most important lesson on discernment in the whole Book of Acts is that prejudice and the stubborn will are larger threats to discernment than insensitiveness and ignorance will ever be.[7]

PRINCIPLE 5 - NEW MUSICAL FORMS DO NOT AUTOMATICALLY MAKE OLD FORMS OBSOLETE

Technology suggests that new is better than old, and old models should be abandoned in favor of (purchasing) new ones. Unhappily, that view also suggests youngsters are better than oldsters, and knowledge is better than wisdom and experience. To suggest that everything traditional is obsolete because there is a new repertoire of musical styles in current use, is to encourage discontinuity with the past—a very dangerous trend that is a relatively new thing. This trend, enhanced by the highlighting of equality at the expense of authority, has succeeded in setting the generations at odds with each other. Unchecked, it could lead to denuding museum walls of the Rembrandts in favor of the Picassos and Pollacks. To subscribe to an either/or mentality in situations where both/and is called for suggests immaturity.

PRINCIPLE 6 - THE GOSPEL CAN AND SHOULD BE EXPRESSED THROUGH MANY MUSICAL STYLES AND CANNOT BE LIMITED TO FIT INTO ANY ONE STYLE

One style of music (rock, waltz, march, gavotte, fugue, etc.) cannot adequately reflect the whole Gospel. To keep things in proper perspective, remember we neither advertise "Christian *Waltz* Concerts" nor "Christian *March* Concerts."

The notion of Christianity as the army of Christ fits nicely with four-quarter time (march style). The gentleness of our Savior and His role as the Good Shepherd find a good accompaniment in three-quarter time (waltz style). Excitement and insistence is portrayed nicely by a fast six-eight time signature when it is beat in two instead of six. Rock-like music can accompany the message of the hopelessness and despair of a life without Christ, and the call for repentance. Rock is insistent, attention-getting, and repetitious. That's not a bad way to get unbelievers to sit up and take notice of the bankruptcy of their lives without Christ.

The trumpet blast of heralds is simple and attention-grabbing. It attracts even the least musical sophisticates. And there is nothing wrong with that! Let the fanfare sound; it has a vital role to play. When it has accomplished its purpose, then it is time to move on to the purpose for which the undivided attention was requested.

PRINCIPLE 7 - IN VIEW OF ROCK'S PAST HISTORY AND ITS PARTICULAR MUSICAL STYLE, IT SHOULD BE USED BY CHRISTIANS WITH GREAT CAUTION!

Do Christians want to protest something the Bible clearly says they ought to protest? Then use a rock or rock-like number. **CAUTION:** Christians need to beware of falling into the same trap that ensnared the members of the counter-culture who in frustration at not being heard, "lost their cool" in rebellion, and called on their peers to do likewise. Mature Christians deal with deaf ears by exercising patience and understanding, not with tantrums nor with loud music.

If Christians want to attract the attention of younger people, especially the 'hard of hearing' (figuratively speaking), then let them try this musical style to gain attention to a new and more transcendent lifestyle. I repeat: once their attention has been obtained, quit hollering! Call for their attention and then give them the message of Christ in a style that reflects the peace of God promised in the Gospel message and with lyrics easily and clearly understood. Then there will be growth into the fullness of Christ.

Let musical accompaniment support and enhance lyrics. If it is boredom, fear, and the frenzy of life without Christ, or if it is the horrors of hell, or spiritual warfare, use the rock style! Just remember to do as the Apostle Paul did who "*fully* proclaimed the Gospel of Christ."[8]

Rock is a highly charged music and it ignites the emotions. We object to highly emotional preaching, calling it "hell-fire and brimstone." Now we are witnessing highly emotional "Christian rock concerts." Indeed, Christians ought to become exercised about sin. There was and still is a place for hell-fire and brimstone preaching! We need more of it today!

Let there be an emotional appeal to persuade sinners to listen and to persuade them to repent! Older evangelicals had no problem with that principle when it came time for altar calls!

Our appeal for help when a fire breaks out may border on the hysterical, but that does not make it immoral! But a whole concert of such a musical style? No! That brings into play other dynamics that are not too healthy.

St. Paul "reasoned" with non-believers in the book of Acts. When reason is lost in an emotional presentation whether in sermon delivery, at the altar call or during a musical concert, we may well question the kind of converts we are making.

PRINCIPLE 8 - *CROSSOVER BY CHRISTIAN ARTISTS WHO LACK DISCERNMENT IS A RELATIVELY EASY STEP TO TAKE AND THE MIXED SIGNALS THAT CAN RESULT CONFUSE BELIEVERS AND NON-BELIEVERS ALIKE*

Christian artists like Amy Grant and Michael W. Smith both made national news when they crossed over to do secular music. When Smith crossed over, *The Wall Street Journal* expressed astonishment on page one! Monica Langley's rather lengthy piece does little to calm the fears of evangelicals about rock and rock-like music. She wrote:

> [Smith] is, in fact, at the vanguard of a trend. . . being signed on by the same big record companies that saturate the airwaves with satanic speed metal and misogynist [women-hating] rap. It is a crossover movement as tricky as it is potentially lucrative. . . It gives them [Smith and a handful of other Christian stars] the awkward job of staking out a middle ground between sacred and profane.[9]

The columnist speaks of a non-biblical "middle ground" and reports that Smith made a "chastely steamy video," that his new record company checked out his concerts before the crossover to make sure "he wasn't handing out Bibles," and that Smith now says, "I know if I'm too blatant about my Christianity and talk about Jesus I won't succeed in the mainstream. But hey, I'm not an evangelist, I'm a singer." She also reports that many of Smith's new fans had no idea he was a gospel singer at all. She notes that he, along with "another hot gospel performer, Amy Grant, acted as host of VH-1's Top 20 Countdown show. . . sponsored by Budweiser."

In light of our study, Amy Grant and Michael W. Smith crossed over long before any formal announcement.

Since all of the Gospel cannot be 'poured' into the rock musical style, any musician who settles for that style in hopes of proclaiming the Gospel must throw away parts of the message that do not fit. The result? Another Gospel. Two of Amy Grant's vocal collections published in the early 1980's are extremely weak on Christology, a trend we are witnessing in our present day. Church leaders, beware!

The Christian message is now decidedly compromised and the secular community is confused. The driving desire to 'make it big,'

sell lots of records and pack out concerts; the willingness to compromise the message; and lucrative offers to go "mainstream" and
sing for secular labels are strongly tempting to Christian musicians.
George Washington is reported to have said, "Few men have virtue
to withstand the highest bidder."[10]

In the *Journal* article, the writer notes that gospel musicians
have been "tilting toward secular idioms" for at least a decade in
order to get played more frequently on the air. She quotes John
Styll, president of the Gospel Music Association who acknowledged
this trend: "The gospel music industry began copying secular acts in
an attempt to get others to see the light; the music was the bait in
fishing for souls." The *Journal* staff writer comments, "This has
stretched the definition of gospel." Alas, how true.

One fan of the new Michael W. Smith buying the first album distributed after the crossover was surprised to learn that this was
Smith's seventh album. On learning the other six were contemporary
Christian records, the 20-year old college student replied, "I don't
believe in religion. I'm into an anthropological view, but hey, that's
cool. I still like [his] music." Whether or not Smith owns up to the
confusion his crossover has caused, the reporter does it for him
when she says. "The *internal* contradictions of his new stardom. . .
don't seem to bother Mr. Smith."

PRINCIPLE 9 - SOME SECULAR MUSICAL TECHNIQUES ARE NOT ADVISABLE

Although many professional Christian artists have already borrowed some of the following techniques, I believe they are in error
and the reasons are obvious:

- Pronunciation that make words sound slushy and indistinct:
  Christian lyrics should come across loud and clear (often
  the problem is simply lack of training);
- Vocal or electronic techniques which distort sound (for example, flatting the sound): the Gospel sets forth life without
  distortion in Christ;
- A bath of the loud dynamic overwhelming the listener and
  conveying a false sense of power, and (along with rhythm)
  inducing a hypnotic state;

- Harmonies that are brash, abrupt, and final chords that are unresolved (left dissonant) except to describe what life is like without Christ;
- Music that fades away at the end of a song (thanks to electronics) suggesting a lack of achievement and finality;
- Rhythm that induces sensual body movements or any other behavior unbecoming a Christian—short skirts or tight pants and a sway of the hips and pelvis draw attention away from Christ and to things very unworthy of the Gospel;
- Any mantra-like patterns of hypnotic repetition (including the repeating of a single chorus or refrain many times over) encourages self-preoccupation and not Christ-preoccupation;
- Any musical style too closely related to an overt world view life-style (problem of association);
- Any program of music that suggests all of the Christian message can be expressed by one musical style;
- Shaking one's head in a 'no' gesture while singing a positive 'yes' Christian message (often done to convey intensity);
- Grimacing (a gesture of pain employed by secular vocalists to indicate intensity) while conveying the message of God's love and peace.

PRINCIPLE 10 - CHURCH MUSICIANS SHOULD PRESENT THEMSELVES IN PUBLIC MINISTRY AS WELL-PREPARED AS THEY EXPECT THEIR PASTOR-TEACHERS TO BE

Here are some suggestions for Christian musicians:

- Pray concerning your selection. Even without specific directions from the pastor or music director, a musician can add immeasurably to worship by being in tune with the same Holy Spirit to whom the pastor and others participating in the service are listening. The service will have a sense of 'oneness' even when total freedom of selection is permitted.
- Never offer to play, sing, or direct the music without reminding yourself first that no matter how well-trained or how well-prepared you are, the presentation or performance

must occur "in the Spirit" and each occasion must be an opportunity to rely on the power of the Spirit rather than on one's skill and poise. This conscious reliance on the Spirit for performance and delivery must never get old.

● Do not go before others without preparing. I will not use the word 'never' since there will certainly be opportunities for spontaneous sharing. However, throwing something together the last minute (except in situations beyond your control) suggests sloppiness and a casualness that is unacceptable in approaching God. A more informal service format must not be an excuse for a sloppy, unprepared frame of mind when approaching the Almighty!

● Singers must articulate as clearly as possible. Words have meaning and it is important to convey biblical truth without ambiguity. Most untrained singers need coaching. Test: have someone listen to a song they are unfamiliar with and report whether or not the words are heard clearly.

● Be willing to 'upgrade' by getting whatever helps are available, including professional coaching whenever possible, especially to learn how to breathe and articulate correctly. *Just as churches budget for pastors to upgrade by attending seminars or take additional college-level training, so churches should budget something for volunteer musicians they use on a regular basis.* Without some skilled coaching, budding musicians (1) may allow poor or sloppy techniques to become ingrained habits; (2) may have only secular artists as role models; and (3) may become quite touchy defending their own immature musical presentations.

● Let the church make an investment in training especially for choir directors—who can instruct the choir members on vocal techniques during choir practices.

PRINCIPLE 11 - BORROWING MUSICAL STYLES FROM THE WORLD IS PERMISSIBLE BUT ONLY WITH GREAT CAUTION (DISCERNMENT)

The following observations are important to consider before deciding to borrow music from the secular culture: Wholesale borrowing from the secular culture will keep the unbeliever from recognizing clearly there are two distinct world views: his own and Christian. Such borrowing can be a deterrent to evangelism not a help. (Success is not measured by how many go to an altar, but how genuine the conversion really is.)

- Using secular music styles with Christian words is appropriate when the musical style clearly supports and enhances the lyrics, the music and lyrics are in agreement, and association is not a problem.
- Since truly Christian music reflects a Christian world view, borrowed secular tunes may require some adjustment or rearrangement to reflect the Christian world view.

PRINCIPLE 12 - *LYRICS SHOULD APPEAL TO THE MIND AS WELL AS TO THE HEART (EMOTIONS)*

"How can they believe in One of whom they have not heard? And how can they hear without someone preaching to them?"[11] The prophet Isaiah reports God as saying to Israel, "Come, let us reason together."[12] Never should preaching or singing be so caught up in emotional wrappings that the appeal of the Word of the Lord to the mind is obscured.

The Word of the Lord, whether in verbal or vocal form, must connect with the will, and the path to the will is both rational and emotional. When the latter takes precedence, inhibitions are shed, the mind is put on hold and the decision made is often regretted in the morning. Music is a vehicle for communicating a greater sense of God-consciousness; *it is not an end in itself.*

CONCLUSION

There has been much change in church music over the centuries, *and there always will be.* Schaeffer's work entitled, *How Should We Then Live?*[13] might be tailored for this study to read, *How Should We Then Sing?* Or, *How Should We Then Play?* I trust I have given some answers to those questions.

The key to a balanced, Christian body of art is balanced, maturing Christian lives. The problem is not resolved by stamping out rock or any other musical style. Nor will it help much to have a record and cassette bonfire. Bringing children to maturity emotionally, intellectually and especially spiritually, will teach them to handle complexity, and the desire for a more balanced menu of musical styles will result. This is primarily the responsibility of the home with assistance from the church and, hopefully, the society. Maturing adults don't forget nursery rhymes, but they outgrow them. Until a believer's world view is more completely formed, thought patterns will tend to go to extremes, and artistic tastes will remain more simple.

How can a parent, distressed over a teen's love for and probable addiction to rock, work with the child? Remember, teens have feelings and in some way, rock is a reflection of their feelings. Forbidding the playing of rock in the home may deal with overt behavior, but not the feelings. Here are some practical guidelines for teens and parents:

- Limit the time: 20-30 minutes at most which must be offset by listening to some other musical style—or turn off the radio, stereo or CD player (principle: moderation).
- If the teen is listening to rock in his room, the vibration of the bass must not be heard coming through the ceiling or the walls to annoy people in other parts of the house (principle: courtesy, love).
- If there is no one at home but the teen, he may turn up the volume, but he must not annoy the neighbors with the pulsating beat (principle: courtesy, love).
- The teen must assume some responsibility in the home such as chores or obligations and personal devotions to earn the right to entertain himself with his music—and the entertainment comes *after* caring for his responsibility (principle: entertainment is a reward for hard work rather than a right or an escape from reality).
- Copies of all lyrics must be supplied to the parents who retain veto over what will or will not be played in the home, and music vetoed will be done so after the parent takes time to explain what Christian principles are violated by the lyrics.

- Walkmans should be forfeited if the sound level is not kept at an agreed level.

One of Schaeffer's statements bears repeating: "The problem is not outward things. The problem is having, and then acting upon, the right world view—the world view which gives men and women the truth of what is."[14] In his addendum, "A Special Note," Schaeffer's emphasis on *knowing* may be somewhat of a lone voice in this age of feeling, but it is the call of a prophet:

> As Christians we are not only to *know* the right world view, the world view that tells us the truth of what *is*, but consciously to *act* upon that world view so as to influence society in all its parts and facets across the whole spectrum of life, as much as we can to the extent of our individual and collective ability.[15]

If we are to understand whether Christian artists are truly reflecting a Christian world view or a secular one, we need to do the following:

- Examine carefully what kind of message they are conveying in the songs they write and sing. Read through a collection of the artist's songs. Is there a strong Christ-centered message, for "He is before all things, and in him all things hold together. And He is the head of the body, the church; He is the beginning and the firstborn from among the dead, so that in everything He might have the supremacy."[16]
- Discern the spirit in which they sing or play while being careful that pretty tunes, pleasing lyrics, and a sincere face do not beguile or mislead and result in loss of objectivity. Only a 'spiritual' heart can discern, never a heart in which dwells a critical or envious spirit.
- Does the artist convey balance in his repertoire?
- Read the non-verbal messages (including dress): does the artist use techniques which support the Christian message or betray it?

The church must come to the realization that our world, characterized by fragmentation, distortion, discontinuity, and dissonance to a frightful degree, needs neither the seniors' 'old order' nor the boomers' and busters' 'new order' imposed on worship, but a Spirit-led, Jesus-Christ-revolutionary-order which changes minds and feelings. The result will be reflected in truly Christian artistic expressions, whether in music or drama, architecture or furnishings.

If we can *only* identify with one musical style such as "The Farmer in the Dell" and the rest of the nursery rhymes repertoire or with rock or even heavy classical, what are we saying about ourselves? We reveal immaturity, reinforce imbalance, and dilute the Gospel.

A dying world rushing in for a face-lift or a crutch when it needs a heart transplant must be confronted with 'sin, righteousness and judgment to come' by preachers not ashamed of the Gospel, and by a body of church music which reflects both the despair and wickedness of sin and the life-giving message of peace, comfort, and hope.

Yes, we can borrow from the world; and yes, we do not need to invent the "wheel" all over again. And no, we don't need to dispose of all secular music and start over if we are to have a truly Christian hymnody. But a spiritual approach does mean that secular musical styles must be submitted to the Holy Spirit for "renewing" (Romans 12:1-2) and sanctifying just as our minds and feelings must be submitted. It is both beautiful and scary: there is more to music than that which tickles the ear.

> *We have not received the spirit of the world but the Spirit who is from God, that we may understand what God has freely given us. This is what we speak, not in words taught us by human wisdom but in words taught by the Spirit, expressing spiritual truths in spiritual words [and song!]. . . The spiritual [person] makes judgments about all things. . .*
>
> St. Paul to the Corinthian Church[17]

> *And this is my prayer: that your love may abound more and more in knowledge and depth of insight, so that you may be able to discern what is best and may be pure and blameless until the day of Christ, filled with the fruit of righteousness that comes through Jesus Christ—to the glory and praise of God.*
>
> St. Paul to the Philippian Church[18]

Notes

Chapter 1   What's Going On Here?

1. William J. Reynolds and Milburn Price, *A Joyful Sound, Christian Hymnody,* p. 114.

2. *Christianity Today,* April 7, 1989, p. 8.

3. Dated 1601 A.D. See *A New Dictionary of Quotations on Historical Principles,* selected and edited by H. L. Mencken.

4. Lyrics by Johnson Oatman, Jr. (1856-1926) and music by Charles H. Gabriel (1856-1932).

5. The newly crowned king of Judah was Joash, son of Ahaziah; see 2 Kings 11:12 NIV.

6. 1 Thessalonians 5:17 NIV.

7. 1 Kings 18:27 NIV.

8. 1 Corinthians 14.

9. Acts 2:37 NIV.

10. July, 1967.

11. Theodore Roszak, *The Making of a Counter Culture,* 1969, pp. 74-75.

12. For the historical setting, see Vinson Synan, *The Holiness-Pentecostal Movement in the United States,* p. 144.

13. See St. Paul's discussion on food sacrificed to idols, 1 Corinthians 8.

Chapter 2   Silver Trumpets, Rams' Horns and Tambourines

1. 2 Chronicles 5:13-14 NIV.

2. Exodus 15:20, Judges 11:34, see also Psalm 68:25.

3. I Samuel 16:23 NIV.

4. For example, Psalms, 81, 89, 92, 95, 96, 98, 100, 101, 105, 108, 126, 149, 150.

5. John R. Davis, *Davis Dictionary of the Bible.*

6. See Psalms 84, 88, 89, etc.

7. Davis, *op.cit.*

8. 1 Chronicles 15:16 NIV; *alamoth* and *sheminith,* according to the NIV note, were probably musical terms.

9. *Ibid.,* verses 19-22.

10. *Ibid.,* chapter 16, verses 5-6 NIV.

11. *Ibid.,* chapter 16, verses 37-38 NIV.

12. Davis, *op. cit.* Also note 2 Samuel 6:5,14; I Kings 10:12; 1 Chronicles 15, 16.

13. I Kings 1:40 NIV tells us that when Solomon was made king, "All the people went up after him, playing flutes and rejoicing greatly, so that the ground shook with the sound."

14. Davis, *op. cit.*

15. William J. Reynolds and Milburn Price, *op. cit.*, p. 1.
16. Davis, *op. cit.*
17. 2 Chronicles 5:12-13 NIV.
18. Ezra 3:10-13 NIV.
19. New International Version.
20. Kenneth W. Osbeck, *The Endless Song, Music and Worship in the Church*, p. 43.
21. Shultze, Anker, Bratt, Romanowski, Worst, Zuidervaart, *Dancing in the Dark, Youth, Popular Culture, and the Electronic Media*, pp. 44-45.

Chapter 3 Spiritual, Fitting, and Orderly

1. Colossians 3:16 NIV.
2. Acts 16:25-26 NIV.
3. Reynolds and Price, *op. cit.*, p. 3.
4. F. F. Bruce, *The Epistle to the Ephesians*, p. 111.
5. *The International Critical Commentary*, Editors: S. R. Driver, A. Plummer, C. A. Briggs, *The Epistles to the Ephesians and to the Colossians*, p. 164.
6. Present tense in Greek, not aorist.
7. Ephesians 5:19 NIV.
8. Bruce, *op. cit.*, p. 111.
9. Wuest, *Ephesians and Colossians in the Greek New Testament*, p. 128.
10. As found in *Strong's Concordance*, "Greek Dictionary of the New Testament."
11. 1 Cor. 14:15b NIV.
12. The Greek verb *sigao* suggests a demand for cessation of disorder; our English word, "Hush!" suggests the same thing.
13. We are left to guess as to the cause of the disorder, but given the model of the open forum style meeting of services in the synagogues with plenty of give-and-take, the probable separation of sexes in seating as was then done and still is among the orthodox Jews, and given the new-found blessing of equality Christian women experienced because of the Gospel, there was plenty of cause for disorder. Emancipated Christian women may have thought that they could also challenge male speakers, a procedure followed in the synagogues between the men present and a speaker (cf. Mark 3:1-4, 6:2-3, Acts 13:44-45, 18:5-7) and most likely adopted in the early local churches. This was altogether counter to Paul's arguments about the ranking of roles as outlined in 1 Corinthians 11:3, and was no doubt the reasoning behind his statement in 1 Timothy 2:12—"I do not permit a woman to teach or to have authority over a man; she must be silent."
14. 1 Corinthians 14:40 NIV.
15. Exodus 32:17-19 NIV.
16. John 12:32 NIV.

Chapter 4 There Will Be Singing!

1. J. A. Estrup and F. Ll. Harrison, *The New College Encyclopedia of Music,* pp. 527-528.

2. Reported by Walter B. Knight and quoted by Paul Lee Tan, *Encyclopedia of 7700 Illustrations,* p. 877.

3. *Ibid.,* quoted from Harry A. Ironside, p. 440.

4. Chadwick, *op. cit.*

5. *Ibid.,* p. 274.

6. William J. Reynolds and Milburn Price, *op. cit.,* p. 4.

7. *Ibid.,* p. 4.

8. Chadwick, *op. cit.,* p. 275.

9. Reynolds and Price, *op. cit.,* p. 5.

10. Chadwick, *op. cit.,* p. 274.

11. Arius, a theologian and founder of the heresy, was born in Libya in 256 A.D. and died in Constantinople in 336 A.D.; he was excommunicated in 311 A.D. because of his heretical views.

12. Reynolds and Price, *op. cit.,* p. 5, quoted from *Music in the Middle Ages* by Gustave Reese, p. 68.

13. *Ibid.,* p. 6.

14. *Ibid.,* p. 10.

15. *Ibid.,* p. 5.

16. *Ibid.,* p. 6. The authors list as chief 'canon' writers, Andrew of Crete (c. 650-730) and John of Damascus (died c. 780). These three forms—troparion, kontakion, and canon—continued in use in the Eastern church for many centuries.

17. *Ibid.,* pp. 7-8. The authors note that by the end of the 4th century there were three basic styles of church music: the responsorial psalm singing (leaders singing what we might call stanzas with congregational response — much like the Old Testament singing at the dedication of the first and second temples), the antiphonal psalm singing, and the metrical hymn.

18. See Reynolds and Price, *op. cit.,* pp. 8-9; Ruth Ellis Messenger, *The Medieval Latin Hymn,* Washington: Capital Press, 1953, p. 10; and, Winifred Douglas, *Church Music in History and Practice,* revised edition, New York: Charles Scribner's Sons, 1962, p. 37.

19. J. A. Westrup and F. L. Harrison, *The New College Encyclopedia of Music,* p. 424.

20. *Ibid.,* pp. 243-244.

21. *Polyphony* is a style of music consisting of two or more independent melodies juxtaposed in harmony.

22. Homer Ulrich and Paul A. Pisk, *A History of Music and Musical Style,* p. 5.

23. Reynolds and Price, *op. cit.,* p. 13.

24. Charles Wesley's hymns totaled some 6,500; Fanny Crosby's total has been placed at 8,000.

25. Reynolds and Price, *op. cit.,* p. 13, quoted from *Liturgy and Hymns,* Vol. 53 of *Luther's Works,* Ulrich S. Leupold, editor; p. 36.

26. Quoted by Edwin Liemohn, *The Chorale: Through Four Hundred Years of Musical Development as a Congregational Hymn,* p. 12; also quoted by Reynolds and Price, *op. cit.,* p. 14.

27. Carrell and Clayton's *Virginia Harmony,* 1831.

28. Reynolds and Price, *op. cit.,* p. 14.

29. 'Macaronic' indicates a mixture of two languages—Latin and the vernacular.

30. Reynolds and Price, *op. cit.,* p. 14.

31. Michael Praetorius, *Syntagma musicum, I* (Wolfenbuttel, 1615); see *Music in the Western World, A History of Documents,* selected and annotated by Piero Weiss and Richard Taruskin, pp. 103-104.

32. Reynolds and Price, *op. cit.,* see pages 89-90.

33. Westrup and Harrison, *op. cit.,* p. 117.

34. Robert D. Harrell, *op. cit.,* pp. 18-19; Harrell is more specific: "15 chorales were composed by Luther himself, 13 came from Latin hymns of Latin service music, 2 had originally been religious pilgrims' songs, 2 are of unknown origin, and one came directly from a secular folk song."

35. *Ibid.,* pp. 21-22.

36. *Ibid.,* pp. 6-7.

37. See Harrell, *op. cit.,* p. 21 and Harrell's source, Archibald T. Davison, *Church Music: Illusion and Reality,* pp. 42-43.

38. Ulrich and Pisk, *op. cit.,* pp. 163-164.

39. *Ibid.*

40. *Ibid.*

41. See Reynolds and Price, *op. cit.,* pp. 16f, and Erik Routley, *The Church and Music,* p. 125.

42. *Homophony* is a style of music consisting of melody with chordal accompaniment, the style of contemporary hymns and gospel songs.

43. See Reynolds and Price, *op. cit.,* p. 17.

Chapter 5 ... And More Singing!

1. Albert Schweitzer, *J. S. Bach,* I, 39.

2. *Op. cit.,* p. 39.

3. *Op. cit.,* Preface to the First Edition, p. vii.

4. *Op. cit.,* p. 43.

5. Short meter has the following number of syllables per line of music (one syllable per note): 6, 8, 6, 6; long meter has 8, 8, 8, 8; and common meter has 8, 6, 8, 6. Example of short meter: "I Love Thy Kingdom, Lord"; example of long meter: "Jesus Shall Reign"; example of common meter: "Amazing Grace."

6. James Lightwood, *Hymn-Tunes and Their Story,* p. 122; quoted by Reynolds and Price, *op. cit.,* p. 46.

7. John Spencer Curwen, *Studies in Worship-Music,* p. 12.

8. Reynolds and Price, *op. cit.,* p. 47.

9. *The Encyclopedia Americana,* Vol. 23, p. 656.

10. *Leadership, Vol. XIV, Number 2,* p. 24; the church is located in Mission Viejo, California.

11. Reynolds and Price, *op. cit.,* p. 58.

12. *Ibid.*

13. *Ibid.,* pp. 82, 94.

14. Well-known for his many gospel songs including, "Wonderful Words of Life."

15. L. E. Jones, Hope Publishing Co., Owner.

16. Copyright 1982 by Maranatha! Music, and WORD Music.

17. Copyright 1974 and 1978 by Mr. Smith.

18. Copyright 1981 by Maranatha! Music.

19. Copyright 1976 and 1981 by Maranatha! Music.

Chapter 6   Felt Life

1. Calvin, *Geneva Psalter* of 1543 (Preface), see also Piero Weiss and Richard Taruskin, *Music in the Western World, A History in Documents,* p. 107.

2. H. R. Rookmaaker, *Art Needs No Justification,* pp. 42, 53.

3. Westrup and Harrison, *The New College Encyclopedia of Music.*

4. Suzanne K. Langer, *Problems of Art,* p. 15.

5. See *Webster's Ninth New Collegiate Dictionary.*

6. Shultze *et al., op cit.,* "Zappa Meets Gore," p. 287; see Calvin Seerveld, *Rainbows for the Fallen World: Aesthetic Life and Artistic Task,* p. 27.

7. Rose Rosengard Subotnik, *Developing Variations, Style and Ideology in Western Music,* p. 9.

8. Shultze *et al., op. cit.,* p. 286.

9. See note 1.

10. H. R. Rookmaaker, *Art Needs No Justification,* pp. 9-10.

11. *Ibid.,* p. 11.

12. Shultze *et al.,* op. cit., p. 147.

13. Adobe Illustrator©, Adobe Photoshop™ (Advertisement).

14. Langer, *op. cit.,* p. 112.

15. *Ibid.,* p. 6.

16. *Ibid.,* p. 9.

17. *Ibid.,* p. 25.

18. *Ibid.,* p. 26.

19. *Ibid.,* p. 8.

20. *Ibid.,* pp. 25-26.

21. Leopold Eidlitz, *The Nature and Function of Art, More Especially Architecture.*

22. Shultze *et al., op. cit.,* p. 151.

23. James M. Riccitelli, this premise was the major hypothesis of my mas-

ter's thesis, *Musical Taste and Social Experience: An Examination of Factors Related to the Enjoyment of Hard Rock and Heavy Classical Music Among Students,* The University of Toledo (Ohio), March, 1978; this quote and subsequent quotes relating to Martindale, Etzkorn, Merriam, etc. are found in chapter 1.

24. *Ibid.*

25. Fredric Rissover and David C. Birth, editors, *Mass Media and the Popular Arts,* p. 254.

Chapter 7 My World, My Music

1. Francis A. Schaeffer, *How Should We Then Live? The Rise and Decline of Western Thought and Culture,* p. 19.

2. H. R. Rookmaaker, *Art Needs No Justification,* p. 12.

3. *Ibid.,* p. 45.

4. Schaeffer, *op. cit.,* p. 19.

5. Francis A. Schaeffer, *Art & the Bible, Two Essays,* pp. 36-38.

6. Sire, *op. cit.,* p. 17.

7. Subotnik, *op. cit.,* 1991; Professor Subotnik, a musical scholar and cultural critic, was appointed Associate Professor of Music at Brown University in 1990.

8. *Ibid.,* p. 3.

9. *Ibid.,* p. 99.

10. *Ibid.,* p. 100.

11. *Ibid.*

12. See Colossians 1:15-20.

13. Subotnik, *op.cit.,* p. 15.

14. *Ibid.*

15. William Ernest Henley, *Rhymes and Rhythms, 25, For England's Sake.*

16. The 1995 Grolier Multimedia Encyclopedia.

17. Schaeffer, *How Should We Then Live,* p. 196.

18. *Ibid.,* p. 199.

19. *Ibid.*

20. James Sire, *op. cit.;* see chapter 3 for further discussion.

21. R. J. Rushdoony, *Intellectual Schizophrenia,* Nutley, N. J.: Presbyterian & Reformed, 1951, p. 12.

22. New International Version.

23. Martindale and Reidel, 1958: Introduction.

24. Etzkorn, 1964: pp.101-107.

25. Etzkorn, 1973: pp. 8-9.

26. Flacks, 1971: p. 61.

27. Jesus said, "You have heard that it was said, 'Do not commit adultery.' But I tell you that anyone who looks at a woman lustfully has already committed adultery with her in his heart." Matthew 5:27-28 NIV.

28. See Romans 12:1-2.

29. This was true in July, 1990, when the author and his wife made a trip

to Quito, Ecuador.

30. Horst de la Croix and Richard G. Tansey, *Gardner's Art through the Ages, Volume II Renaissance and Modern Art (8th Edition)*, pp. 3, 6.

31. Schaeffer, *How Should We Then Live*, p. 184.

32. *Ibid.*, p. 184.

33. *Ibid.*, p. 98.

34. *Ibid.*

35. *Ibid.*, p. 193.

36. *Ibid.*, p. 187.

37. Rookmaaker, *Art Needs No Justification*, pp. 47-48.

Chapter 8   The New Musical Style: Rock

1. K. Neill Foster, *The Discerning Christian, How to identify near-truth and avoid its increasing peril*, p. 29.

2. H. R. Rookmaaker, *Modern Art and the Death of a Culture*; Rookmaaker, now deceased, was professor in History of Art at Amsterdam's Free University.

3. Hall and Ulanov, *Modern Culture and the Arts*, essay by Ulanov, *"What is Jazz?"* pp. 114-121.

4. *Ibid.*, p. 116.

5. Quoted by Howard and Lyons, *op. cit.*, p. 115.

6. Howard and Lyons, *op. cit.*, p. 113.

7. Marshall Stearns, *The Story of Jazz*, p. 80.

8. Carl Belz, *The Story of Rock*, p. 33.

9. Christine Ammer, *Harper's Dictionary of Music*, pp. 300-301.

10. *Ibid.*

11. James D. Graham, "Rhythm in Rock Music," *Popular Music and Society*, pp. 33, 37-38.

12. Paddy Whannel and Stuart Hall, "The Young Audience," in *Modern Culture and the Arts*, p. 143.

13. I will use 'form' and 'structure' interchangeably. Form, according to Westrup and Harrison, *op. cit.*, "means intelligible shape. The basic elements in musical form are (1) repetition, (2) variation, (3) contrast (whether of material, of speed, or of dynamics). . . These three principles operate in the field of (a) melody, (b) harmony, (c) rhythm, (d) tone-color. . ." p. 216.

14. Gene Grier, *The Conceptual Approach to Rock Music*, p. 39.

15. *Ibid.*

16. *Ibid.*, p. 10.

17. Shultze *et al.*, *op. cit.*, p. 151 and p. 148.

18. *Ibid.*, p. 149.

19. Carl F. Seashore, *Psychology of Music*, p. 142.

20. *Op. cit.*, p. 143.

21. James M. Riccitelli, "The Tempo of Beat Music and Its Implications Relative to Behavior."

22. Curt Sachs, *Rhythm and Tempo: A Study in Music History*, p. 332.

23. Seashore, *op. cit.*, p. 142.

24. *Ibid.*, p. 138.

25. *Ibid.*

26. Langer, *op. cit.*, pp. 126-127.

27. Seashore, *op. cit.*, p. 148.

28. *Ibid.*, pp. 140-145.

29. Quoted in *Encyclopedia of 7700 Illustrations, Signs of the Times*, p. 898.

30. Richard J. Fogarty, *Rock, the Quiet Revolution*.

31. Vernon M. Albers, *The World of Sound*, p. 59.

32. From an unpublished paper by James M. Riccitelli, "The Implications of Rock'n'Roll as a Cultural Factor in Morbidity," 1971; the Nader information appeared in local newspapers in The Toledo Blade (newspaper), 7-21-69.

33. So reported by Hildebrand, *Columbia Law Review*, 1971.

34. Janet Rotter, *Glamour Magazine*, under the by-line, "Sound," Nov. 1968.

35. Benjamin DeMott, "Rock As Salvation," *Pop Culture in America.*, pp. 199-200.

36. The Greek verb *pletho* means "'to fill" as does the verb *pleroo* (found in Ephesians 5:18 in connection with 'spiritual fruit,' and elsewhere in the New Testament), but the former word, used in connection with 'spiritual gifts,' carries with it the meaning of 'control'; this latter word is used often in the Book of Acts, e.g., in Acts 2:4 and in 13:9 where we read, "Then Saul, who was also called Paul, filled with [*pletho*, "controlled by"] the Holy Spirit, looked straight at Elymas, and said. . ." (NIV).

37. DeMott, *op. cit.*, p. 266.

38. *Ibid.*, p. 199.

39. *Ibid.*, p. 21.

40. James D. Graham, "Rhythm in Rock Music," *Popular Music and Society*, p. 37.

41. Michael Zerwin, "Fancy Rock," in *Mass Media and the Popular Arts, op. cit.*, p. 284.

42. See Riccitelli, "The Tempo of Beat Music," *op. cit.*

43. Dated 1969, p. 29; see Riccitelli Thesis, *op. cit.*, p. 22.

44. *Op. cit.*, p. 143; see Riccitelli Thesis.

45. *Op. cit.*, pp. 36-41.

46. Ephesians 4:15.

47. Grier, *op. cit.*, p. 1.

Chapter 9 Rock: Do We or Don't We?

1. 1 Corinthians 10:23 NIV.

2. Bob Larson, *Rock, Practical Help for Those Who Listen to the Words and Don't Like What They Hear*, pp. 92-93.

3. Taken from: *The Endless Song, Music and Worship in the Church*, by Kenneth W. Osbeck, © 1987, Kregel Publications, Grand Rapids, Michigan. Kregel Publications. Used by permission, p. 105.

4. *Ibid.*, p. 106.

5. *Ibid.*, pp. 107-108.

6. *Ibid.*, pp. 108-109.

7. Lawrence J. Crabb, Jr., *Effective Biblical Counseling*, pp. 47f.

8. Exodus 12:35-36: Crabb refers to the account of the Israelites as they prepared to leave Egypt; they took the Egyptians' silver, gold and clothing—given freely by the Egyptians we might add—and left everything else behind.

9. See Numbers 11:5.

10. 1 Corinthians 8:4 NIV.

11. 1 Corinthians 8:9 NIV.

12. Weiss and Taruskin, *op. cit.*, page 107.

13. *Ibid.*

14. Hall and Ulanov, *op. cit.*, *Modern Culture and the Arts*, pp. 83-87, "The Appalling Popularity of Music."

15. *Ibid.*, p. 87.

16. See 1 Kings 19:12.

17. 1 Corinthians 14:8.

18. In speaking of order in worship in 1 Corinthians 15 (NIV), Paul touches on these principles: verse 12, "Since you are eager to have spiritual gifts, try to excel in gifts that build up the church"; verse 26, "When you come together, everyone has a hymn, or a word of instruction, a revelation, a tongue or an interpretation. All of these must be done for the strengthening of the church"; verse 40, "But everything should be done in a fitting and orderly way."

19. *Webster's Ninth New Collegiate Dictionary.*

20. 1 Cor. 1:23-24.

21. Lyrics by Charlotte Elliott (1789-1871), music by William B. Bradbury (1816-1868).

22. See 1 Samuel 6:20.

23. Weiss and Taruskin, *op. cit.*, p. 103.

24. A transcultural study would be most interesting. The same view of fast and slow music is apparent among many of the tribes of West Africa.

25. So reported by *Time Magazine* some twenty or more years ago.

26. Weiss and Taruskin, *op. cit.*, p. 104.

27. See Piero Weiss and Richard Taruskin, *op. cit.*, p. 105. They attribute this "oft-quoted remark" to Luther, but give no reference. Their statement obscures what Luther composed and hoped for.

28. Piero Weiss and Richard Taruskin, *op. cit.*, p. 103.

29. *Webster's Ninth New Collegiate Dictionary.*

30. See R. G. Moyles, *The Blood and Fire in Canada, A History of the Salvation Army in the Dominion 1882-1976*, pp. 37-43, "The Songs They Used to Sing" (Chapter 4).

31. *Ibid.*, p. 40.

32. The accompanying paper containing the lyrics for this cassette entitled

"David Meece" says, "Special Thanks to Monster Cable. . . For Correspondence and Information on concerts & concessions please write: David Meece Productions, P. O. Box 1605, Franklin, TN 37065-1605."

Chapter 10   Setting Boundaries

1. Galatians 5:22-23 NIV.
2. 1 Corinthians 10:31 NIV.
3. 2 Corinthians 3:18 NIV.
4. Gospel of John 8:29 NIV.
5. Acts 2:23, 37-41 NIV.
6. William L. Hooper, *op. cit.,* p. 60.
7. Foster, *op. cit.,* p. 90.
8. Romans 15:19 NIV.
9. *The Wall Street Journal,* Wednesday, September 11, 1991, Vol. LXII, No. 231.
10. Paul Lee Tan, *op. cit.,* p. 618.
11. Romans 10:14 NIV.
12. Isaiah 1:18 NIV.
13. This title is based on Ezekiel 33:10.
14. Schaeffer, *How Should We Then Live?* p. 254.
15. *Ibid.,* p. 256.
16. Colossians 1:17-18 NIV.
17. 1 Corinthians 2:12, 13, 15 NIV.
18. Philippians 1:9-11 NIV.

Bibliography

Adams, Jay. *Marriage, Divorce and Remarriage in the Bible,* Grand Rapids, Michigan: Baker Book House, 1980.

Albers, Vernon M. *The World of Sound,* South Brunswick & New York: A. S. Barnes & Co.; London: Thomas Yoseloff, Ltd., 1970.

Ammer, Christine. *Harper's Dictionary of Music,* New York: Harper & Row, Publishers, 1972.

Anderson, Leith. *Dying for Change, An Arresting Look at the New Realities Confronting Churches and Para-Church Ministries,* Minneapolis, Mn. 55438: Bethany House Publishers, 1990.

Apel, Willi; Daniel, Ralph T. *The Harvard Brief Dictionary of Music,* New York: Washington Square Press, 1960.

Bailey, Albert. *The Gospel in Hymns,* New York: St. Martin's Press, 1955.

Barna, George. *User Friendly Churches, What People Need to Know about the Churches People Love to Go to,* Ventura, California: Regal Books, a division of GL Publications, 1991.

Barna, George. *What Americans Believe, An Annual Survey of Values and Religious Views in the United States,* Ventura, California: Regal Books, a division of GL Publications, 1991.

Belz, Carl. *The Story of Rock,* New York: Colophon Books, 1969.

Blom, Eric V. editor. *Grove's Dictionary of Music and Musicians,* 5th edition, New York: St. Martin's Press, 1955, "Luther."

Bruce, F. F., *The Epistle to the Ephesians,* London: Pickering & Inglis Ltd., 1961 (1968).

Calvin, John. *Geneva Psalter* of 1543.

Carrell and Clayton's *Virginia Harmony,* 1831.

Cassou, Jean et al., *Art and Confrontation, The Arts in an Age of Change,* Greenwich, Connecticut: New York Graphic Society Ltd. (translated from the French by Nigel Foxell), © 1968 in Belgium by La Connaissance S. A.

Chadwick, Henry. *The Early Church,* The Pelican History of the Church - I, England: Penguin Books, 1967.

Crabb, Lawrence J., Jr., *Effective Biblical Counseling,* Grand Rapids, Michigan: Zondervan Publishing House, 1977.

Curwen, John Spencer. *Studies in Worship-Music,* London: J. Curwen & Sons, 1880.

Davis, John R. *Davis Dictionary of the Bible,* Grand Rapids, Michigan: Baker Book House, 1955.

Davison, Archibald T. *Church Music: Illusion and Reality,* Cambridge:
    Harvard University Press, 1952.
De la Croix, Horst; Tansey, Richard G. *Gardner's Art through the Ages,
    Volume II Renaissance and Modern Art,* San Diego & New York:
    Harcourt Brace Jovanovich Publishers, (1926) 1986.
Douglas, Winifred. *Church Music in History and Practice,* revised edition,
    New York: Charles Scribner's Sons, 1962.
Driver, S. R.; Plummer, A.; Briggs, C. A.; Editors. *The International Critical
    Commentary, The Epistles to the Ephesians and to the Colossians,*
    Edinburgh, 1952.

Easton, M. G. *The Illustrated Bible Dictionary,* New York: Crescent Books, 1989.
Eidlitz, Leopold. *The Nature and Function of Art, More Especially
    Architecture,* NY: A. C. Armstrong & Son, 714 Broadway, 1881; reprint-
    ed, New York: DaCapo Press, 1977.
Emurian, Ernest K. *Living Stories of Famous Hymns,* Grand Rapids, Michigan:
    Baker Book House, 1955 (Interlude Books).

Fogarty, Richard J. *Rock, the Quiet Revolution,* Schroon Lake, New York:
    Word of Life Fellowship, Inc., 1972.
Foster, K. Neill. *The Discerning Christian, How to identify near-truth and
    avoid its increasing peril,* Harrisburg, Pennsylvania: Christian Publications,
    Inc., 1981.

Gardner, Helen. *Art through the Ages, An Introduction to Its History and
    Significance,* New York: Harcourt, Brace & Company, 1926.
Graham, Billy. *The Jesus Generation,* Grand Rapids, Michigan: Zondervan
    Publishing House, 1971.
Graham, James D. "Rhythm in Rock Music," *Popular Music and Society,* Vol.
    1, No. 1, Fall, 1971.
Grier, Gene. *The Conceptual Approach to Rock Music,* Valley Forge,
    Pennsylvania: Charter Publications, 1974.

Hall, James B.; Ulanov, Barry; editors. *Modern Culture and the Arts,* New
    York: McGraw-Hill, Inc., 1957.
Halverson, Richard. *How I Changed My Thinking about the Church,* Grand
    Rapids, Michigan: Zondervan, 1973.
Harrell, Robert D. *Martin Luther, His Music, His Message,* Greenville, South
    Carolina 29606, P. O. Box 6524: Musical Ministries.
Hayford, Jack. *Worship His Majesty,* Waco, Texas: Word Books, 1987.
Hooper, William L. *Ministry & Musicians, The role of ministry in the work of
    church musicians,* Nashville, Tennessee: Broadman Press, 1986.
Howard, John Tasker; Lyons, James. *Modern Music, A Popular Guide to
    Greater Musical Enjoyment,* A Mentor Book, New York and Toronto:

The New American Library, 1957, originally published by the Thomas Y. Crowell Company in hardback.

Jahn, Mike. *Rock, From Elvis Presley to the Rolling Stones,* Chicago: New York Times Book Company: Quadrangle Books, 1973.

Kroll, Woodrow. *The Vanishing Ministry,* Grand Rapids, Michigan: Kregel Publications, 1981.

Langer, Suzanne K. *Problems of Art,* New York: Charles Scribner's Sons, 1957.

Larson, Bob. *Rock & Roll, the Devil's Diversion,* McCook, Nebraska: Bob Larson, 1967, 1970 (revised edition).

Larson, Bob. *Rock & the Church,* Carol Stream, Illinois: Creation House, 1971.

Larson, Bob. *Rock, Practical Help for Those Who Listen to the Words and Don't Like What They Hear,* Wheaton, Illinois: Tyndale House Publishers, Inc., 1980.

Leupold, Ulrich S. editor. *Liturgy and Hymns,* Vol. 53 of *Luther's Works,* Philadelphia: Fortress Press, 1965.

Liemohn, Edwin. *The Chorale: Through Four Hundred Years of Musical Development as a Congregational Hymn,* Philadelphia: Muhlenberg Press, 1953.

Lightwood, James. *Hymn-Tunes and Their Story,* London: The Epworth Press, 1923.

Lomax, John A.; Lomax, Alan; Seeger, Ruth Crawford (music editor). *Our Singing Country, A Second Volume of American Ballads and Folk Songs,* New York: MacMillan Company, 1941.

Lystad, Mary. *As They See It, Changing Values of College Youth,* Cambridge, Massachussets: Schenkman Publishing Company, General Learning Press, 1973.

Marshall, Madeleine. *The Singer's Manual of English Diction,* New York: G. Schirmer, 1953.

MacArthur, John F., Jr. *Ashamed of the Gospel: When the church becomes like the world,* Wheaton, Illinois: Crossway Books, a Division of Good News Publishers, 1993.

Martindale, Dan; Riedel, Johannes; Neuwirth, Gertrude; editors. *The Rational and Social Foundations of Music,* Southern Illinois University Press, 1958.

McLuhan, Marshall. *Understanding Media,* McGraw-Hill Company, 1964.

Mellers, Wilfred. *Music in a New Found Land: Themes and Developments in the History of American Music,* New York: Alfred A. Knopf, 1967.

Mencken, H. L., editor. *A New Dictionary of Quotations on Historical Principles,* New York: Alfred A. Knoff, 1966.

Messenger, Ruth Ellis. *The Medieval Latin Hymn,* Washington: Capital Press, 1953.

Moyles, R. G. *The Blood and Fire in Canada, A History of the Salvation Army in the Dominion 1882-1976,* Toronto, Canada: Peter Martin Associates Limited, 1977.

Noebel, David A. *Rhythm, Riots and Revolution,* Tulsa, Oklahoma: Christian Crusade Publications, 1966.

Osbeck, Kenneth W. *The Endless Song, Music and Worship in the Church,* Kregel Elective Series, Grand Rapids, Michigan: Kregel Publications, 1987.

Pinnock, Clark H. *Set Forth Your Case, Studies in Christian Apologetics,* Chicago: Moody Press, 1971.

Praetorius, Michael. *Syntagma musicum, I* (Wolfenbuttel, 1615), New York: DaCapo Press, 1980.

Reese, Gustave. *Music in the Middle Ages,* New York: W. W. Norton & Company, 1940.

Reich, Charles A. *The Greening of America,* New York: A Bantam Book, 1971.

Reynolds, William J.; Price, Milburn. *A Joyful Sound, Christian Hymnody,* New York: Holt, Rinehart and Winston, 1978.

Riccitelli, James M. *Musical Taste and Social Experience: An Examination of Factors Related to the Enjoyment of Hard Rock and Heavy Classical Music Among Students,* The University of Toledo (Ohio), March, 1978.

Rissover, Fredric; Birth, David C.; editors. *Mass Media and the Popular Arts* (A Reader), N. Y.: McGraw-Hill, Inc., 1971.

Rookmaaker, H. R. *Art Needs No Justification,* Downers Grove, Illinois: Inter-Varsity Press, 1978.

Rookmaaker, H. R. *Modern Art and the Death of a Culture,* Downers Grove, Illinois: InterVarsity Press, 1970 (third edition, 1973).

Roszak, Theodore. *The Making of a Counter Culture,* Garden City, New York: Doubleday and Company (an Anchor Book), 1969.

Rushdoony, R. J. *Intellectual Schizophrenia,* Nutley, New Jersey: Presbyterian & Reformed, 1951.

Saint Augustine Confessions, trans. R. S. Pine-Coffin, London: Penguin Books, 1961.

Sachs, Curt. *Rhythm and Tempo: A Study in Music History,* New York: W. W. Norton and Company, 1953.

Schaeffer, Francis A. *How Shall We Then Live, The Rise and Decline of Western Thought and Culture,* New Jersey: Fleming H. Revell Company, 1976.

Schaeffer, Francis A. *Art & the Bible, Two Essays,* Downers Grove, Illinois: InterVarsity Press, 1979.

Schaeffer, Francis A. *Escape from Reason,* Downers Grove, Illinois: InterVarsity Press, 1968.

Schaeffer, Francis; C. Everett Koop, M.D. *Whatever Happened to the Human Race? Exposing our rapid yet subtle loss of human rights,* Tarrytown, N.Y.: Fleming H. Revell Company, 1979.

Schafer, William. *Rock Music: Where It's Been, What It Means, Where It's Going,* Minneapolis, Minn.: Augsburg, 1972.

Schweitzer, Albert. *J. S. Bach*, New York: Macmillan Co., 1950.

Seashore, Carl E. *Psychology of Music*, N.Y.: Dover Publications, Inc., 1938, 1967 (Dover edition).

Seeger, Ruth Crawford. See Lomax, John A.

Seldes, George. *The Great Quotations*, Secaucus, New Jersey: Castle Books, 1977.

Shultze, Quentin J., Project Director; Anker, Roy M., Project Editor; Bratt, James D.; Romanowski, William D.; Worst, John William; Zuidervaart, Lambert. *Dancing in the Dark, Youth, Popular Culture, and the Electronic Media*, Grand Rapids, Michigan: William B. Eerdmans Publishing Company, 1991.

Sire, James. *The Universe Next Door*, Downers Grove, Illinois: InterVarsity Press, 1977.

Stearns, Marshall. *The Story of Jazz*, New York: Mentor Books Reprint, originally published by Oxford Press, 1958.

Stedman, Ray C. *Body Life, the Church comes alive*, Glendale, California: Regal Books, Gospel Light Publications, 1972.

Stott, John R. W. *Balanced Christianity*, Downers Grove, Illinois: InterVarsity Press, 1975.

Strong, James. *Strong's Exhaustive Concordance of the Bible*, McLean, Virginia: MacDonald Publishing Company.

Subotnik, Rose Rosengard. *Developing Variations, Style and Ideology in Western Music*, Minneapolis, Minnesota: University of Minnesota Press, 1991.

Synan, Vinson. *The Holiness-Pentecostal Movement in the United States*, Grand Rapids, Michigan: Eerdmans, 1972.

Tan, Paul Lee. *Encyclopedia of 7700 Illustrations*, Rockville, Maryland: Assurance Publishers, 1984.

Ulrich, Homer; Pisk, Paul A. *A History of Music and Musical Style*, New York: Harcourt, Brace & World, Inc., 1963.

Weinberg, Steven. *The First Three Minutes: A Modern View of the Origin of the Universe*, New York: Bantam Books, 1976.

Weiss, Piero; Taruskin, Richard. *Music in the Western World, A History of Documents* (selected and annotated); New York: Schirmer Books (Div. of Macmillan, Inc.), 1984.

Westrup, J. A.; Harrison, F. L. *The New College Encyclopedia of Music*, revised by Conrad Wilson, New York: W. W. Norton & Co., 1976.

White, David Manning; editor. *Pop Culture in America*, Chicago: Quadrangle Books (A New York Times book).

Wuest, Kenneth. *Ephesians and Colossians in the Greek New Testament*, Grand Rapids, Michigan: Wm. B. Eerdmans Publishing Co., 1954.

ARTICLES

Adobe Illustrator©, Adobe Photoshop™ (Advertisement).

DeMott, Benjamin. "Rock As Salvation," *Pop Culture in America,* David Manning White, editor; Chicago: Quadrangle Books (A New York Times book).

Graham, James D. "Rhythm in Rock Music," *Popular Music and Society,* Vol. 1, No. 1, Fall 1971.

Riccitelli, James M. "The Implications of Rock'n'Roll as a Cultural Factor in Morbidity," 1971; the Nader information appeared in The Toledo Blade (newspaper), 7-21-69. (unpublished)

Riccitelli, James M. "The Tempo of Beat Music and Its Implications Relative to Behavior," Toledo, Ohio: The University of Toledo, Department of Sociology, Anthropology and Social Work (unpublished).

Weber, Max. Essay, "The Rational and Social Foundations of Music"; see Martindale and Reidel.

Whannel, Paddy; Hall, Stuart. "The Young Audience," in *Modern Culture and the Arts,* a reader edited by James B. Hall and Barry Ulanov, New York: McGraw-Hill, Inc., 1957.

Zerwin, Michael. "Fancy Rock," in *Mass Media and the Popular Arts,* New York: McGraw-Hill Book Company, 1971.

JOURNALS

Christianity Today, April 7, 1989.

Columbia Law Review, 1971.

Journal of the American Medical Association 262, Sept. 1989.

Leadership, A Practical Journal for Christian Leaders, Vol. 14, No. 2, Spring, 1993, published by *Christian Today,* Inc., Carol Stream, Illinois.

Mass Media and the Popular Arts (A Reader), N. Y.: McGraw-Hill, Inc., 1971.

Popular Music and Society, Vol. 1, No. 1, Fall 1971.

Practical Anthropology, Vol. 9, Number 6, November-December 1962 (special issue, "Developing Hymnology in New Churches"), William A. Smalley, editor.

MISCELLANEOUS

Webster's Ninth New Collegiate Dictionary, Springfield, Mass.: Merriam-Webster, Inc., 1989.

The Enclyclopedia Americana, Vol. 23.

Hymns of the Christian Life, Harrisburg, Pa.: Christian Publications, Inc., 1978 (The Christian & Missionary Alliance).

Bible, New International Version, Indianapolis, Indiana: B. B. Kirkbride Bible Co., Inc. and Grand Rapids, Michigan: Zondervan Bible Publishers, 1983.

Bible, Today's English Version (Good News), copyright 1976, American Bible Society.

Praise Chorus Book, "Jesus, I Love You," by Monroe Thompson, Costa Mesa, CA: Maranatha! Music.

The 1995 Grolier Multimedia Encyclopedia.

NEWSPAPERS

The New York Times, Special Feature, May 29-30, 1971, "Sounds of the Seventies," column by Mike Jahn.

The Toledo Blade, July 21, 1969.

The Wall Street Journal, Vol. LXXII, No. 231, Sept. 11, 1991.

VIDEO

Riccitelli, James M. *The Meaning of Salvation, Paired Values.*

JAMES M. RICCITELLI is a graduate of Nyack College (Nyack, N.Y.) where he majored in theology, and the University of Toledo (Ohio) where he earned both bachelor's and master's degrees in sociology. His master's thesis was entitled, "Musical Taste and Social Experience: An Examination of Factors Related to the Enjoyment of Hard Rock and Heavy Classical Music among Students."

Ordained by the Christian and Missionary Alliance, Mr. Riccitelli pastored churches in West New York, N.J., and Sidney, N.Y., and served as a three-term Alliance missionary along with his wife, Ruth, and family, in Burkina Faso, West Africa. There he engaged in church planting and development; reduction to writing of the language of the tribe formerly called Red Bobo (now, Bwa); director of the Christian bookstore and the radio ministry, and pastor of the French language services. His article on linguistics (tone reduction) was published by the United Bible Societies, articles on ethnomusicology were published by Practical Anthropology, and an article on education from a Christian perspective was published by the College of Education of the University of Toledo. He is also a musician and continues to compose music for church use.

After returning from the mission field, he served as minister of music at First Alliance, Toledo, Ohio and interim pastor of the First United Presbyterian Church in Toledo. He then became founding pastor of the Berean Fellowship of the Church at Toledo (now affiliated with The Christian and Missionary Alliance) where he is in his twenty-third year as pastor. He taught as adjunct professor at the University of Toledo, Adrian College (Adrian, Michigan), Detroit Bible College, Toledo Extension (later called Toledo's Center for Biblical Studies), and William Tyndale College (Farmington Hills, Michigan).

Mr. Riccitelli also has a counseling ministry and ministers as a conference speaker. He is committed to Biblical solutions to social—especially, relational—problems.